ENLIGHTENMENT AND ILLUMINATION

SPIRITUAL WISDOM FROM
DJWAHL KHUL

CHANNELED THROUGH
DAVID J ADAMS

authorHOUSE®

AuthorHouse™
1663 Liberty Drive
Bloomington, IN 47403
www.authorhouse.com
Phone: 1 (800) 839-8640

Published by AuthorHouse 06/12/2019

ISBN: 978-1-7283-1253-8 (sc)
ISBN: 978-1-7283-1251-4 (hc)
ISBN: 978-1-7283-1252-1 (e)

Library of Congress Control Number: 2019942658

Print information available on the last page.

The Front cover Picture of the 8 Pointed Spiral Star Labyrinth of Creation was painted and photographed by Kaye Ogilvie, Queensland, Australia, from a design Channeled though David J Adams.

Back cover Photo was taken on the camera of David J Adams, the T shirt was created by Tie Dye artist, Ruth Cary Cooper from USA.

DEDICATION

I Dedicate this book to my children, Nicky and Suzi, my grandchildren, Lauren, Matthew and Emily, and my great grandchildren, Ruby–Rae and Peyton, for they and others of the next generations will carry the Light forward and create the Peace that we all yearn for.

ABOUT THE AUTHOR

ADAMS, David John Patrick

Born: 28th April 1943

At: Mountain Ash, Glamorgan, South Wales, UK.

Moved to South Australia in 1971, Currently living in the southern suburbs of the city of Adelaide.

Began his Spiritual Journey as a result of the Harmonic Convergence in late 1987.

In 1991, he was asked by Beloved Master Germain to undertake a global Meditation based on, and working with, the Consciousness of the Oceans, which was called the Marine Meditation.

In 2009 he was asked to address a Peace Conference in Istanbul to speak of the Marine Meditation and his work for World Peace through meditation.

He is a Songwriter, a Musician, an Author and Channel, but most of all a **SERVANT OF PEACE**.

David began bringing through information from a variety of Masters and Cosmic Beings in the form of Meditations around 1991. It was not, however, until after the year 2000 that he began to channel messages in group situations and in individual sessions. Most of these messages were not recorded or transcribed so remain shared with only a few people, but in 2009 the messages being brought through in the weekly Pendragon Meditation group began to be recorded and transcribed by Kath Smith and sent out around the world on David's own Pendragon network.

David's special Guide and Mentor has been 'The Germain, the I am that I am', but he has also worked extensively with – and channeled - Sananda, Hilarion, Djwahl Khul, AA Michael, The Merlin, The Masters of Shambhala, as well as Arcturian Sound Master Tarak and his own Home Trinity Cosmic Brother Ar'Ak.

(Contact email – djpadams8@tpg.com.au)

ACKNOWLEDGEMENTS

I, David J Adams, would like to acknowledge three special Earth Angels.

Heather Niland/Shekina Shar - who helped me to awaken to my Journey in 1987 and connected me to my Beloved Friend "The Germain", she was a mentor, guide and teacher way ahead of her time.

Meredith Pope – who walked in the same shoes as me in those difficult early years as a fellow 'weekender' at The EarthMother Centre, and was - and still is - an inspiration to me.

Krista Sonnen – An Harmonic and Earthwalker, who helped to build the bridges to my Spiritual and Cosmic friends by persistently urging me to allow them to speak through me in private sessions, then in group sessions. Without her support these messages would not be here.

I would further like to acknowledge **Kath Smith** – A spiritual Being of immense Love and Joy who initiated the recording and transcribing of the messages received in Pendragon so that the messages from our 'other Dimensional friends' would not be lost forever. Also **Takara Shelor,** who combined her Global Water Dolphin Meditation with the Marine Meditation in 1998 and has organized the Marine Meditation website as an adjunct to her own Dolphin Empowerment website ever since. Also **Kaye Ogilvie**, Intuitive Spiritual Artist, who Painted all the Labyrinths walked during the Marine Meditations, as well as many other inspirational images that have assisted my Journey of Growth.

I also acknowledge all those here in Australia and those throughout the World who have supported me and encouraged me over the years, and in particular**, Barbara Wolf and Margaret Anderson**, who's vision and hard work has made this book possible.

BLESSINGS OF LOVE, JOY AND PEACE TO EACH AND EVERY ONE OF YOU.

DAVID J ADAMS

FOREWORD

We Humans live in the concept of "Linear Time', which divides 'Time' into minutes, hours, days, months, etc. and goes in a straight line from 'Past' through 'Present' to 'Future', consequently we give importance to the date on which something happens. Our Spiritual and Cosmic Friends are not bound by such constraints, they operate in the **'Now'** moment, so although the messages within this book have 'dates' attached to them, they are, essentially, **TIMELESS**.

Some messages do, of course, refer to specific events, such as the Equinox or the Solstice, or even some man made event, however, the underlying message is always **TIMELESS**. So we ask, when you read these messages, that you accept them as having importance within the **'Now Moment'** of your lives. Although we have given the date of receipt at the end of each message, they are not in sequential 'linear time' order.

All messages were received within the Pendragon Meditation Circle and always began with the 'Sounding" of the Tibetan Bowls, the Blessings Chimes, the Drum, and occasionally other percussion instruments. Many of the messages make reference to these Sound frequencies.

Let the messages speak to your Heart, for that is what they were intended to do when they were given by **DJWAHL KHUL**.

Blessings of Love, Peace and Joy

David J Adams

INTRODUCTION

Djwahl Khul, sometimes referred to as 'The Tibetan', began working with me in 1999 when he and Master Hilarion formed a Trinity of Masters with Beloved Germain to continue to work on the Global Marine Meditation that Beloved Germain had instigated with me in 1991. The Meditation designed to connect Humanity with the Consciousness of the Oceans and all the Beings of Light within the Oceans. From time to time he would come through me as an individual Master and gift Humanity with words of Wisdom, as well as working with me as part of the Council voice of the Masters of Shambhala.

Many of his words of Wisdom were lost to Humanity – as were words of Wisdom from other Masters and Cosmic Ambassadors - as they were never recorded and transcribed in the early years. Thanks to the efforts of Kath Smith when she joined the Meditation group in 2008, more recent words of Wisdom have been preserved and are presented here in this book.

His words have always sought to uplift and guide us towards a greater understanding of ourselves in our search for Enlightenment and Illumination, our personal responsibilities and our Community and Global responsibilities.

I hope you will find within the words of his messages in this book an upliftment of Spirit and an enhancement of the Light that **already exists within each one of you.**

Blessings of Love, Peace and Joy.

David J Adams
(djpadams8@tpg.com.au)

CONTENTS

1

BREATH IS A SACRED ENERGY

(The Circle opens with the Sounds of the Tibetan bowls and the Blessings Chimes.)

Embrace the Blessings of Sound and feel those Blessings permeate every part of your Being - feel it, know it, and radiate it forth out into the world that you may share with others upon this Planet the Blessings within your Heart, for it is so important to acknowledge the Blessings within yourself and to share those Blessings with others through the Sound of the beating of your Heart, through the Sound of your voice, through the Sound of your breath.

You perceive breath as a function of life, *but breath is so much more than that, breath represents the vibrational frequency of your total Being*, it is the giver and the receiver of Blessings, so as you breathe in, you breathe in the Blessings that exist upon the Earth Planet, and as you breathe out, you breathe out the Blessings that exist within your Heart, and when these two things come together you begin to create magical, beautiful happenings upon the Earth, and everything begins with your breath, for *your breath is a frequency of Light,* it is much, much more than the Sound of life, so take a moment now to just breathe and listen to the Sound of Blessings that your breathing carries.

Greetings, Dear Hearts, I am Djwahl Khul and I come to you tonight on your breath, I come as a Blessing, and I come to share, to share the Blessings of all your Spiritual friends and your Cosmic friends, for they are with you tonight, they breathe with you into the centre of this Circle to create a magnificent array of Blessings.

All too often you forget the importance of breath, for you define it within your physical terms, when in fact *breath is a sacred energy,* a sacred energy that you create, a sacred energy that you rely upon to sustain your life, but also to improve your life, for it is through your breath that you change the rhythms of your life. It is through your breath that you embrace higher Dimensional Frequencies. It is through your breath that you draw into yourself the Love and the Light that is cascading onto the Earth at this time from the Cosmos.

Focus on your breath, listen to it, feel it moving throughout the whole of your Being, it is *the Cosmic wind of your Soul* coursing through your bodies, vibrating, creating the Sound of You, the Sound of You both as a physical Being and as a Spiritual Being.

You could say that your breath is your 'umbilical cord to God. It is what binds each and every one of you together into Oneness.

Expand your view on what breath means for you and means for others, for every Being upon your Planet breathes - trees breathe, plants breathe, animals breathe and with that breathing they vibrate, and that vibration sings a peculiar song that belongs to them and yet melds them with all other Beings, for you are all breathing from the same pool of air, from the same Spiritual source and you are contributing to that same pool of air.

THIS is your Oneness, when your mind cannot cope with the understanding of what Oneness really is, bring it back to your breath, and through your breath have the knowing that this is the Oneness you share.

You may have, Dear Hearts, individual physical vessels for your time on this Planet, but within those physical bodies, and exuding from those physical bodies is the breath - That is your Oneness.

Focus again on your breathing, breathing in the Blessings and breathing out the Blessings. Many ancients on your Planet - ancient civilizations, ancient practices, focused for their Spiritual development upon their breath and their breathing, and by becoming *One with their Breath* they found their *Oneness with all that is.*

It is time, Dear Hearts, to remember the wondrous aspect of life that the breath represents. You cannot see your breath, but without it you know you would not exist, it has power and importance way beyond the understandings of your mind.

Breathe in the *Magenta Light* of Earth Mother, Breathe out the *Magenta Light* from your own Heart, and as you do so acknowledge the Oneness of all that is, and know that through your breath you connect with every living Being upon the Earth and beyond the Earth, for *breath is part of the source of all life.*

Breathe yourselves into Higher Dimensional Frequencies and feel yourself being uplifted with every breath you take.

It is time to remember, Dear Hearts –
Focus on your breathing and you will know true Oneness.

(19th October 2015)

2

EACH OF YOU HAS A
DANCE TO DANCE

(The circle opens with the Sounds of the Tibetan bowls and the drum)

Imagine that you are a dragonfly emerging from the waters in which you were born, and unfurling your wings to catch the rays of the sun to dry your body and strengthen your body until you are ready to take to the air and fly, darting hither and thither, dancing through the sunbeams that warm you and fill you with iridescent colour, and you become a Being of infinite colour, infinite movement, and you look out upon the Earth to see which part of the Earth you need to Bless with your colours, for *your purpose on this Planet at this time is to Bless the Earth and all upon it with your colour,* with your many iridescent colours, utilizing the rays of the sun to reflect on your wings and cast a myriad of colours upon the Earth and upon Humanity.

Greetings, Dear Hearts, I am Djwahl Khul.

I hope you enjoyed the imagery of the dragonfly, for that is how you should begin to see yourselves, as Beings of Light and colour casting your Joy upon all of Humanity, upon all Beings of Light upon your Planet.

In every waking moment you can BE the dragonfly, you can move in any direction with infinite lightness, you can communicate with the sun, translating its energies through your wings and blessing the Earth. You have emerged from the waters and become part of the air, a transformation of incredible beauty as you move into different Dimensions of life.

There will be times when you will rest awhile and look around, but then once more you will take flight and you will carry your Blessings to more and more people. Once you have accepted within yourself that this is your role upon this Earth, you are uplifting the Earth and all upon it into the realms of Light, into the realms of Joy.

You will never again return to the water, Dear Hearts, that part of your cycle of life has gone, but it has contributed to the strength within you, to the power of flight, but you now look upon that water as your past, you let go of the bondage of the water and you embrace the sunlight and the air and the breeze, you are flying in higher and higher Dimensions of Light.

A part of you will always remember the womb of water from which you came, but now you are on a new part of your journey, a part that is filled with colour, filled with the rays of the Sun. You are the connection between the Sun and the Earth, weaving threads of Light and colour throughout the Earth, touching the Hearts of ALL of Humanity.

Take a moment, Dear Hearts, and in your Hearts and in your minds allow yourself to *BE* a dragonfly. Feel yourself moving higher and higher, feel the rays of the Sun caressing your wings, being transformed into iridescent colours which cascade down upon the Earth.

This is a time of great transformation upon your Planet, *YOU are central to that transformation, each and every one of you has a role to play. Each one of you has a dance to dance, so now let yourselves dance the dance of Joy, and let your colour bathe the Earth.*

(9th June 2014)

3

THE "HEART TEST"

(The Circle opens with the Sounds of the Tibetan Bowls and the Blessings Chimes)

Greetings Beloveds, I am Djwahl Khul.

I come to speak to you tonight about the *"Heart Test"*. No, Dear Ones, I do not mean a medical examination to see if your valves are working, I speak of the need to move into your Heart and find the Truth that lies within.

Throughout the *'millennia of the mind'* you have worshiped at the altar of proof and fact and logic and reason. All of which are important, but all of which can be manipulated to enslave the bulk of Humanity, and indeed through those millennia, this has often been the case.

Now it is the time, not to 'worship' at the altar, but to *'embrace'* the *"altar of Truth"* within your Hearts, for Truth cannot be manipulated, and Truth cannot be used to enslave the Human spirit. It is time to let go of that 'millennia of the mind' and to begin a new *'millennia of the Heart'*.

It is important to embrace the Truth within your Hearts, and although logic and reason and proof and facts can all be utilised in discovering Truth, it is only within your Heart that you *know* Truth, and knowing is much more than being convinced.

You may recall, Dear Ones, we have said at the beginning of this year that from time to time we would bring again to you "pearls of wisdom" that were gifted to you before. In this instance, I refer to the words of Beloved Ar'Ak – Spirit Brother of this one - when he came to you and said

"Proof is not a measure of reality.

Proof is a measure of the level of one's own scepticism".

It may be that you did not understand what that meant at the time, so I ask you again to feed that through your Heart and ask for the Truth of it to be revealed to you. It is saying to you that there is no such thing as proof, for the proof for one person does not convince another, whereas *Truth simply IS. It exists.* It does not need to be proven. It does not need a range of facts to be aligned in order for you to understand it.

You need to move from the mind into the Heart in order to embrace and understand *"Truth"*. Facts, hmmm, how many times, Dear Ones. does something have to be repeated in order for it to be considered "fact"?

It is always wise to think carefully when someone keeps on saying to you that "this is fact", because if you feed it through your Heart and ask for the truth of it, you will see that what is being put before you is often simply an opinion, a belief, not a "fact" at all.

Logic and reason are important, but they too can be utilised and constructed in different ways, by different Beings, and different meanings can be arrived at from the same "facts".

Take for example, the subject of "Global Warming". It is of amazement to us that debate upon your Planet continues about the existence or otherwise of Global Warming, of *'climate change'*.

Dear ones, feed that through your Heart, ask for the Truth of it, and immediately you will know that of course, the climate of the Earth is changing. *It is always changing!* There is no debate. There is no need for proof and facts of this. It is constantly changing, but it suits the purpose of some to continue the charade of debating the pros and cons, of seeking proof that outstrips the proof of others.

Your Heart knows, and your Heart also knows that the Truth will not be heard until the right questions are being asked. You see, it is not a question of whether climate change exists or not. As I say, climate change is constant on your Planet. It has been in a state of change since the beginning of time. It is called *Evolution.*

The question that ought to be addressed at this time Dear Ones, is not whether climate change is real. The question is, "what does each of you do in order to live in harmony with this ever changing Planet?"

Once you accept the Truth within your Heart that climate change is a reality, a constant reality, you do not seek to apportion blame for this change. Change is change. Dear Ones.

Indeed it can be added to by activities of Humanity, or it can be balanced to a degree by activities of Humanity, but these are answers to different questions. The question is 'what can each of you do to *'live in harmony'* with this ever changing world of yours?'

This why I say to you tonight, Dear Ones, it is time to bring the "Heart Test" into your lives, to feed everything you read, everything you see, everything you hear into your Heart, and ask for the Truth of it for YOU.

The Truth for you is what is important. For the Truth for you is what sets out your pathway in the future, for once you embrace the Truth within you, your Light will begin to shine, and you will see more clearly the appropriate pathway for you in this world.

That pathway, Dear Ones, is about harmony. It is about being in harmony with the Earth.

Truth is within your Heart. Feed everything through your Heart, and ask for the Truth of it for you.

There will still be many on your Planet who are worshiping at the "altar of the mind". Do not let that concern you unduly, for they will find the Light within themselves in their appropriate time. Focus on yourselves. Focus on the Truth within your Heart.

Your Truth will enable you to ask the right questions. When you ask the right questions, you receive the answers from within your own Heart - the answers of Truth – not of right or wrong, but of Truth.

I ask you to consider this, Dear Ones. ***Embrace the Truth within your Hearts.***

I thank you and I bless you.

(9th April 2012)

4

RESPECT AND HONOUR ALL OTHERS

(The Circle opens with the Sounds of the Tibetan Bowls and the Drum)

Feel the vibrations of Love swirling around the Circle, connecting each and every Being of Light within the Circle with the strands of Love. Feel yourself becoming empowered by this energy of Love, and feel yourself expand - moving beyond the Circle to embrace the whole of the Earth, and the whole of the Universe in your Circle of Love.

Greetings Dear Hearts, I am Djwahl Khul.

This one was not too keen to accept us tonight, (*because of my cough !*) but still we have decided to come through to speak with you again.

This is a time of great change upon your Planet, as you have been told so many times before, and during times of change it is not easy to see the ways ahead, for as you look out upon your Planet you see confusion and chaos, you see the darkness within Humanity coming to the surface, and you may ask yourself 'Where is the Light that we have been promised, that we have been told is coming to this Earth in greater and greater amounts?'

I say to you, Dear Hearts, it is this very Light that is allowing you to see the darkness that needs to be shifted within Humanity.

In past times you would have been mainly in ignorance of what is happening on your Planet, for much has been concealed, but now as more and more Light shines upon the Earth Planet, everything is coming into view, giving each and every one of you the opportunity to discern what is appropriate for you, what you are prepared to accept in the new Earth, and what you will let go.

What you are seeing, Dear Hearts, is an *'absence of respect'*, respect for each other's individuality, respect for each other's beliefs, respect for each other's differences, and you are being shown this, Dear Hearts, in order that you may embrace it with Love, and then let it go. For in a Dimension of Oneness there is no room for an absence of respect, there needs to be a greater understanding that each and every Being upon the Earth is unique, is worthy, is necessary.

Think about that a moment, Dear Hearts, it is all too easy to judge and to reject, simply because others views are different to yours, but the Dimension of Oneness is one in which you *respect the differences of others, and you embrace the uniqueness of each and every individual*, and when I speak of individuals I do not necessarily mean only Humanity,(*cough*), I speak also of the creatures of the Oceans, for you are seeing at the moment a movement by many, many people who are standing up and saying *'We must respect the creatures of the Ocean, they have a role to play on this Planet, they are valued'*. There are still those who do not respect the creatures of the Ocean, who continue to regard them as in some way a threat to Humanity, but as you will have seen on your TV screens there are many, many, many, people all around the world who are standing tall and speaking from their Hearts and saying *'We are One with the beautiful Creatures of the Ocean'*.

The last vestiges of fear are being brought to the surface for you to see, and for you to let go, for there is no place for fear in the *New Earth*, in the new Dimension of Oneness, where you *respect and honour all others*.

So, instead of focusing on the few that continue to disrespect your brothers and sisters in the Ocean Dimension, focus instead on the many that are speaking out, opening their Hearts, standing tall alongside their brothers and sisters, for in the end, Dear Hearts, *respect will outweigh the fear*, and you will come to understand and embrace with great Love all the creatures of the Ocean.

Humanity has a wonderful way of delineating, of determining that one creature is acceptable, but another is not. That judgment is invariable based on fear, so let go of fear, embrace the totality of your Earth, the Ocean creatures, the creatures of the air - *all* have a part to play.

Embrace all.
Love all.
Accept all.

Here in this Circle you live beside the Ocean, reach out, embrace your brothers and sisters in all their forms, and no longer let fear determine which creature you accept and which you reject.

Embrace the Oneness and stand tall with all other open Hearts and say to the world

'We will no longer live in fear; we accept and embrace ALL upon the planet'.

(3rd February, 2014)

5

GRATITUDE

(The Circle opens with the Sounds of the Tibetan bowls and the Blessings Chimes.)

Greetings Dear Hearts, I am Djwahl Khul.

I am delighted to be with you this evening, and I wish to speak about *'Gratitude'*. You have often been told by your Spiritual friends how important it is to express gratitude in your life, to draw to you abundance in everything, but there is a tendency amongst Humanity, Dear Hearts, to assume that this refers to expressing gratitude for what you receive in your life, when in reality what we are referring to is *expressing gratitude for who you ARE in your life, and for WHAT you are in your life,* for everything around you is an expression of you.

You create the environment around you, so when you are in receipt of something, it is because you have called it to you, and when you express gratitude for the gift you have been given, you are in fact expressing gratitude to yourself for having created the situation that draws - by your energy - that aspect of life into your physical realm.

That is not to say that you should not give gratitude to others, but it is important that you remember that you draw others into your life for the exchange of energy that takes place between you, and when that exchange of energy creates Joy and happiness within you, it is because you have willed that to happen.

It is time, Dear Hearts, for each and every one of you to realize the power that YOU possess, the power that you use every moment of every day of your life to create your experiences. It is true, within your Dimension, the logic of the mind will have, or will create, rational explanations for everything that occurs in your life, but the reality is that You, and You alone command and create the life that you are participating in.

When abundance comes into your life it is because you have called it into your life. I am here tonight to encourage you to acknowledge your power, your own power of creation. This does not put you above anyone else, Dear Hearts, it is simply an acknowledgment of the responsibility you have as a Being of Light upon the Earth to create Wisely, and to be in gratitude for what you are creating.

This may be a slightly different take on your life, and on what gratitude is all about, but it is important for you to recognize and acknowledge and accept the true power within you, for when you do so you open yourself completely to everything, to everyone in your life, you release the barriers of the past. You make no judgement of others because you have called those others into your life for your own purpose, your own growth, your own learning.

You are the centre of your own universe, that is what gratitude is all about, Dear Ones, accepting that you are the centre of your own universe, and the whole world, and the whole Cosmos **IS** your Universe, *there is nothing that lies outside that universe, nothing that lies outside You.* Every feeling, every emotion, every thought exists within you, and manifests externally within your Dimension, for that is the purpose of being on the Earth Planet at this time - to manifest physically that which is within you, the Light and the Love and the Peace that is within you, and you do that by calling into your life, experiences, interactions with other

Beings, interactions with nature, interaction with animals.

All these are yours to command, and all these are reason to continually express your gratitude for the beauty, the wondrous nature, of everything that has been created from within you.

We have often spoken to you of ONENESS, this is the essence of Oneness, that the whole universe exists within you.

I ask you now, take a moment to look out on your life as it is at the moment, of those you are interacting with, of things you are doing, places you are going, all these are chosen by YOU, so when you look out upon your life and you think of making judgments, remember, you are simply judging yourself!

Everything in your life upon the Earth Planet is for the benefit of your growth, of your Ascension; everything is therefore created by you, within you, for that purpose.

I know, Dear Hearts. as Humans you will look out upon your life and you will see things that you do not like and you will think 'I could not possibly have created that', and yet you have, Dear Hearts, *you have created everything for the purpose of your own evolvement, your own growth.*

This is why, Dear Hearts, we speak to you so often, asking you to express gratitude in all you do, in all you feel and all you think,

*for with **GRATITUDE** comes **LIGHT**,*
*and with **LIGHT** comes **LOVE**,*
*and with **LOVE** comes **PEACE**.*

Blessings be upon you, Dear Hearts.

(17th November 2014)

6

ALLOW YOUR HEARTS TO BEAT IN UNISON WITH THE EARTH PLANET

(The Circle opens with the Sounds of the Tibetan Bowls and the Blessings Chimes)

Allow the Sounds of the Bowls and the Blessings Chimes to uplift your Hearts into your Soul Dimension, and within your Soul Dimension connect most powerfully with the Heart beat of Mother Earth, for this is a time of re-connection to the Heart beat of the Planet. A time to let go of the Physicality of your Being, and become immersed instead into the Soul Frequencies of *All that is*, and *'All that is'* is contained within the Heart beat of Earth Mother.

Feel yourself being embraced with the deepest Love that the Earth Planet itself has for all those who share its journey of Ascension. Let go of the perception of your separateness from the Planet, and embrace the essence of Oneness.

Greetings, Dear Hearts, I am Djwahl Khul.

It is **SO** important at this critical time of change that you become an integral part of the Earth Planet itself. Do not see yourselves as walking the surface of the Earth, **Feel** yourself becoming a part of the Earth. Let your Heart Beat resonate with the Heart Beat of the Earth itself. The time of separation has come to an end, more and more of Humanity are opening their Hearts, opening their Minds, connecting to their Souls, and becoming a Conscious part of the Oneness of the Earth Planet.

Dear Hearts, you have worked diligently for a considerable time to move yourselves to this point of **Communion** with the Earth, it is not a time to look back with regret over the pain and suffering that you have created upon the Earth, for this was all a part of the journey. ***It is simply a time to recognize your UNITY, your ONENESS with the Earth Planet, and to allow your Hearts to beat in unison with the Earth Planet.***

There are many, many groups of people on your Planet who look at different aspects of the Earth, and seek to improve their connection with the Earth, all these need now to come into Oneness to no longer seek to be better than, greater than, wiser than, but simply accept that 'Being with' is what counts - *Being with Earth Mother, Being with the Earth Planet, Being with each other - Unity, Comm - Unity.*

There are many clouds across the Earth that take away the Light and the Sound, but those clouds are beginning to thin, and the Light is permeating more and more, showing the way for Humanity, showing the way for ALL the Light Beings on the Earth Planet and within the Earth Planet.

Dear Hearts, as you well know, your Spirit friends tend to chose certain specific events or specific dates on your calendar, to bring their energies to bear to assist you and the Earth in its upliftment, for when more than one person is focused on a particular event or a particular day, the greater the energy is created.

You are now coming up to the day that you call 'Valentine's day', a day that resonates with the word *Love*, and in past years we have asked you to utilize that particular day to send your Love to the Earth. But Valentine's day is more than simply about Love, it is about *expressing* that Love, *communicating* that Love, not only for the Earth but for the rest of Humanity.

I am sure, Dear Hearts, that you will recall in your teen years that Valentine's day had a slightly different meaning, it was a time when you were able to express your Love for someone without them really knowing who you were, (smile), Do you recall that, Dear Hearts ? the simple act of expressing 'feelings' of Love almost anonymously,

I think it is time, Dear Hearts, that you revived that in your lives, so I am here tonight to ask you at the time of your Valentine's day to Express the Energy of Love, to your friends, to your families. Do it in a way that brings laughter and joyfulness, and for each Being this will be a little different. Yes, Dear Hearts, you may say 'Valentine's day' has become just one more commercial enterprise, with cards and flowers and expectations - but, the essence of the day remains the expression of the Love within Your Heart to people who do not necessarily know that you have these feelings of Love for them.

This is particularly so in family situations, ask yourselves, Dear Hearts, when was the last time you told someone in your family that you Love them

? perhaps you have an expectation that they already know that, it is no longer necessary to say these things, it is embarrassing to tell someone within your family that you Love them, but how are they to know unless you communicate, connect, express ? *Love is not something to be hidden within your Heart, it is an energy that needs to be shared. Needs to be expressed for it to come alive, and when Love energies are alive on your Planet, Joy, Happiness, Harmony is created, and more and more Light is created. Many of the clouds that hide your Sun are created by a lack of communication of Love.*

So perhaps, Dear Hearts, I can ask you on this coming Valentine's day to reach out to members of your family, to your friends, and be prepared to express the Love that is within your Hearts. Yes, Dear, Hearts, it may well be misunderstood by some, but to remain silent simply because someone may misunderstand, is to bring more and more clouds in front of your Sun, at a time when the World needs more and more sunshine, more and more Light, more and more Love.

You do not need to buy a card, or buy a flower, or make a gift of any kind, you simply need to open your Heart, and open your mouth, and *Express the Love that is within you,* in so doing you are not expecting anything in return. You do not need for that person to come back to you and say that they Love you, that does not matter, what is important is that you begin to express freely the Love within your Heart. *I am sure, Dear Hearts, that you will be amazed at the Joy that this will bring, and the Light that this will create,*

Valentine's day, the whole world *IS* your Valentine, the Earth *IS* your Valentine, but whilst you may not be able to communicate that Love to people the other side of the world, there is nothing, nothing at all, to stop you from expressing that Love to those closest to you. So when you awaken on this Valentine's day, take a moment to decide who it is that you are going to contact and connect with on that day, and -

EXPRESS THE LOVE IN YOUR HEART !

(2nd February 2015)

7

NOTHING ON THIS EARTH IS OUTSIDE YOUR CONTROL

(The Circle opens with the Sounds of the Tibetan Bowls, the Blessings Chimes and the Drum)

Just relax and breathe deeply. Immediately focus upon the perfection of your own Being. Embrace that perfection. Embrace the Light within that perfection.

Feel yourself immediately becoming uplifted in Spirit, for as you embrace the perfection of self,
   You let go of the denser energies,
   You let go of the fears,
   You let go of the doubts,

You embrace the perfection of your own Being.

Greetings, beloveds, I am Djwahl Khul.

I am here tonight to tell you in no uncertain terms that there is nothing, and I repeat, nothing happening on your world that is not within your control !

Think on that a moment. You have been told many times of the powerful energies that are flowing into your Planet at this time – *energies for creating change.* But these energies continue to be just energies until they are focused with the *Intent of manifestation,* and that, Dear Ones, can only be done by you.

So there is no point in looking out to those energies and saying "What is happening to me?" – Nothing is happening to you !

You have the opportunity in every moment of every day to create your reality by working WITH these energies of powerful change.

Perhaps I could use a simple analogy – When you think of your electricity that runs along the lines outside your homes, and then down the lines and into your homes, they are just energy - they have no purpose, they have no effect until you, with your intent, create a focus. You may do that by simply switching on a light, and suddenly the electricity becomes Light. Or you may turn on your kettle, and suddenly the electricity becomes a means by which you heat your water.

You see, it is your intent and focus which creates from this energy.

When you think of it in those terms Dear Ones, you will see why I began by saying *"Nothing is happening in your World that is out of your control"*

You, each and every one of you – You are the Creators.

You are the ones through whom this energy will be focused with intent.

Through *Your* intent the energy becomes manifested in creation.

That is a powerful responsibility, Dear Ones, it is imperative that your focus is from the highest level of your Being.

The lower energies still exist on your Planet. They too can tune in to this energy, and through this energy, and through its focus, create more of the lower energy frequencies.

But that is your choice. What you create with these powerful energies depends on your individual, and collective choices.

The more individual Humans who create through Divine Love, the more the collective Consciousness of Humanity will begin to create through Divine Love.

Do not look outside yourselves. It is your choice to connect to the energies that are flowing to the Earth, and to create with those energies from the highest source of your Being.

Your choice in every moment of every day is creating the new reality of Earth.

The energies in and of themselves are simply ENERGY. They will flow to and through the Earth until they are harnessed and focused into *CREATING*.

> Nothing on this Earth is outside your control
> Remember that, Dear ones,
> Nothing is outside your control.

If, of course, you perceive yourself as being totally separate from all the rest of Humanity, you may find that statement difficult to accept, difficult to embrace. But, of course, you are not separate from the rest of Humanity, nor indeed are you separate from the rest of the Dimensions within your Planet, and upon your Planet. You are all part of the ONE.

So, your choices, your decisions. your focus, not only relates to you, they relate to the Whole. Equally, the decisions of others impacts upon you, for you are a part of the Whole.

So again I say to you – ***"Nothing on this Earth is outside of your control"***

Move into your Hearts, Dear Ones, move into your state of Perfection, and as you embrace the energies flowing into the Earth at this time, Focus those energies, bring more and more Light into the Earth, and into Humanity.

You have the choice, and you have the responsibility, to ***BE*** the ***PERFECTION THAT YOU ARE.***

I bless you, and thank you for all your efforts to this time.

I embrace you with the Deepest Love

Choose wisely, Dear Hearts.

And so it is.

(25th April 2011)

8

YOU WILL CREATE MAGICAL CHANGES UPON YOUR PLANET

(The Circle opens with the Sounds of the Tibetan Bowls and the Blessings Chimes)

The resonance of the Balmaceda Bowl calls out to your Heart from the Temple of Divine Oneness, embracing you with the energies of Love, the energies of Unity. Imagine the vibration of the Bowl flowing across the Earth Planet, awakening the Light in everyone's Heart, calling them into the Oneness of themselves, and the Oneness of the Human Consciousness.

Greetings Dear Hearts, I am Djwahl Khul and I come tonight to embrace you and thank you - each and every one of you - not only within this Circle tonight, but those from across the Earth who came together at the Equinox to create another step in the significant changes taking place upon the Earth Planet.

The amazing Light that you together created across the Earth shifted the Planet into a new orbit of Oneness within its Ascension journey. Each time you come together and join your Hearts as ONE, you impact the journey of the Earth Planet.

You called upon the Consciousness of the Oceans to carry your Light of Love across the Earth and it did so. It empowered many powerful Sacred Sites throughout the Earth, both within and without the Ocean Consciousness.

The flow of Light and Love around the Earth raised great celebrations within the Cosmos as the whole Earth became alight with a new glow of Unity, a new vibration of Oneness.

There will be a short period within your linear time for these new energies to become absorbed fully by the Planet, and stabilize in readiness for the next gigantic step forward into Cosmic Stardom, and within each of your physical bodies you will need to adjust and find a new equilibrium to match the new vibrational frequencies.

Take your time, go inside and find that point of stillness within yourself and feel the Love within you, embrace the Love within you, and shine forth the Love within you.

See yourself each day as a part of the whole, not giving of your energies as you did in the past, but simply sharing in the energies of the Oneness of all that is.

Within that sharing of Oneness you will create magical changes upon your Earth. Giving and receiving was a part of the old duality, now, Dear Hearts it is simply the time of sharing, of becoming the Oneness, and within the Oneness to create your own unique Light that gives resonance and colour to all around you.

There are more steps to be taken between now and the time of the Great Shift that has been prophesized, but you will be ready for each and every one of those steps, for you have committed to the journey, you have committed to the Earth at this time, and we will walk with you, we will embrace you with our Love, with our Light, with our Warmth and with our Divine Resonance.

We move forward now - together in Oneness.

On behalf on my brother Germain and my brother Hilarion I am honoured to embrace you and thank you once more for the energies you have contributed to the Enlightenment of Mother Earth.

Blessings be

(1st October 2012)

9

LOVE IS THE GREAT CHANGE MAKER

(The Circle opens with the Sounds of the Tibetan bowls, the drum and the tingsha bells.)

As you feel the vibrations of Sound flowing deep into your Heart, imagine that this is the Heart of the Earth speaking directly to you, speaking of the Love that the Unity brings to **all that is**, letting go of all feelings and sensations of separateness, and embracing totally the Sound of Oneness, the simple beat of your Heart, and the Heart of the Earth, becoming **ONE**.

And as you feel the beat of your Heart beginning to create the energies of Joy within you, know that the beat of Earth's Heart is beginning to create the energies of Joy for everyone upon the Earth, for the beat of the Earth's Heart is amplified and communicated through the crystalline structures of the Earth, and these are now reflected in the new crystalline structure of Humanity itself.

Feel the vibration of Oneness, allow yourselves to melt into that vibration, and feel the growth, the expansion of Love within you, and radiating from you. Feel the beat of the Heart of everyone else upon the Earth, for when you beat with the same Heart there can be no separation, there can be no judgements, and there can be no hatred. ***When you beat from the same Heart there is only Love, and THAT is the energy of the New Earth frequencies, Dear Ones, the energies of Love, the energies of Oneness, the energies of Unity.***

It is time to let go of everything that is not Oneness. As you feel your own Heartbeat, know you are feeling the Heartbeat of all - of the Earth itself, of the Cosmos. You are a part of the Oneness. You are the Oneness. In every moment of your daily lives think of your Heartbeat as being the Heartbeat of the Earth. Accept it, and through that acceptance let go of your judgements.

When you look at someone else, feel their Heartbeat, know it is your Heart that is beating within them, their Heart beating within you, for this is the Oneness.

You each have individual contributions to make to the New Earth, the biggest contribution is the acceptance of the Oneness that you all are now in this new Dimensional frequency - *the frequency of Love.*

Change always takes time, so let go of judgements of yourself if you are unable immediately to embrace this new concept of Oneness, if you are unable to look at someone else and feel their Heart beat as your own - allowing yourself to be aware of it is the beginning of that change, and the more you focus upon it, the more it becomes the reality of your life.

Take a moment, open yourself and feel the Heartbeat of everyone else within this Circle. Feel it as your own, hear it as your own, and then *own the Oneness of the magical Circle,* and feel the intensity of the beat of your own Heart as it becomes one with all the others.

You have known for a considerable period of time, Dear Ones, that when you come together, you are vastly more powerful than the sum of the numbers, for when you come together and focus on the same intent, you are beating with the same Heartbeat, for what you are creating with your intent is pure Love, and *LOVE IS THE GREAT CHANGEMAKER, LOVE IS THE GREAT HEALER, LOVE IS EVERYTHING.*

Allow yourselves now to listen to the Heartbeat of the Earth, and allow that to become the Heartbeat within you, and feel yourself being empowered as you expand your understanding of Love, the understanding of the magic that exists within everything, upon and within the Earth.

Love resided within your Heart and is transmitted by your Heartbeat. Embrace it, expand it, become one with the universal Heartbeat.

The time of separation is over, the time of embracing the ONE is upon you. It is for each of you to determine how quickly you embrace the New Earth, how quickly you learn about the Love within yourself, and through the Love within yourself, learn about the Love of *all*.

Be within your Hearts at all times, Dear Ones, for it is within your Heart that you will know the essence of Oneness, and the essence of Joy, and the essence of Peace, and the essence of Serenity.

I am Djwahl Khul and I embrace you with the beat of <u>MY HEART</u>.

(28th January 2013)

10

WHAT YOU FEEL WITHIN YOUR HEART IS WHAT YOU CREATE WITHIN YOUR LIFE

(The Circle opens with the Sounds of the Tibetan Bowls, the Blessings Chimes and the Drum)

Just relax and find a nice comfortable position, let yourself flow easily and gracefully into the centre of your Being. Recognizing that, at this time, it is the centre of your own Being that is your anchoring point.

At this time of change for the Earth Planet, the instability of the Earth within its new Dimensional frequency suggests that you should not anchor yourself into the Earth as you have previously done. When you are looking for balance and stability in your life, allow yourself to flow powerfully into the centre of your own Being, and become anchored within your own Heart.

This does not disconnect you from the Earth itself, it simply allows you to maintain balance within the new Dimensional frequencies, and by allowing you to establish balance within yourself, you enhance the ability of the Earth to create balance and harmony within its new Dimensional frequency.

The Earth needs to become stabilized within the new frequencies, as do each of you. You do it individually, but the effect is collective. For the more that you can balance and anchor yourselves within the deepest part of the centre of your Being, the more balanced the energies you then radiate forth into the Earth, assisting the Earth, assisting yourselves.

So focus your intent at this time to create stability and balance within your Being. Feel the flow of energies from deep within your Heart Chakra radiating forth, embracing every atom of your Being, establishing a Sacred Space with the Higher Frequencies of Divine Love and Divine Peace.

Feel the completeness of your Selves. Feel the flow of that energy opening you to all that is, opening you to the energy of others, to the energies of the Earth, to the energies of the Cosmos, remaining constantly in balance and Harmony within yourself.

The energies at this time are fluid. This can be disconcerting if you are not in balance within yourself. So it is imperative at this time to be in balance – the balance that is a natural state of Being within each one of you. *You do not need to force it, you just need to allow it to be.*

You are going back to the womb of time, not the womb of your physical Being, but the womb of your energy Being.

You are a harmonious spark of Light, and the fluid movement of energy throughout the Cosmos. When you feel that you are a part of the natural flow of energy, you lose your disconnection with all that is. You become once more a part of the whole.

You may think that being a part of the whole means that you lose a part of your identity, but that is not so, you find your identity within the flow of Cosmic energies, because you acknowledge the balance and harmony within your Centre.

Imagine for a moment that your energy Being is a balloon floating through the air, self contained, yet moving with the energies of the Cosmos. Allow yourself to flow freely, guided by your Inner

Voice, feeling completely free and yet completely belonging.

The freedom is within your uniqueness, but it is also within your togetherness. When you sit balanced in the Centre of your Being, you can expand, and expand, and expand, to where you are eternal.

Embrace the Love, embrace the Peace, allow yourself to flow, allow yourself to be part of the flow. Let your energies within this circle move freely around, embracing, intermingling harmoniously, one with the other and with your surroundings, with the many Energy Beings of Light that share this space with you tonight. Feel the Love, feel the Peace, feel the Serenity of being at the centre of your Heart.

I am the one you call **Djwahl Khul**, and I honour each and every one of you here tonight, and share with you the flow of **MY** energy, as do all your friends in other Dimensional frequencies, for we are all **ONE,** balanced, Harmonious, flowing in Love and Peace.

Although this may not seem, on the surface, to be reflected on your Planet at this time, know that it is so, and focus your intent, focus your Being, on

Love and on Peace, and see those energies flow throughout the whole of your world. Everyone upon your Planet, and within your Planet, will be caressed by this flow of loving, peaceful energy, and they will be influenced and changed by the embrace of these energies.

So do not look upon the negative aspects of your Planet at this time, accept simply to note that they exist, but look instead at all the positives, at all those instances in your life where Love and Peace prevail, and give your energy to those aspects of Life upon your Planet. Support that which is good with your energy. Understand when things are not so good, but do not criticize or judge, simply give more of your Love and Peace energies to the flow of the Earth, and the Earth will itself become more stabilized and harmonious within its new frequencies of Love and Peace, and all upon it will be affected by the flow of those energies.

Focus in your Heart, embrace all Beings upon your Planet from the Love within your Heart.

Allow your friends in other Dimensions to join with you as you work tirelessly to stabilize the Earth in its new frequency. *Be open to the Pearls of Wisdom they may gift to you from time to time, directly into your Hearts.*

What you feel within your Heart is what you create within your life. Feel the Love. Feel the Peace, and Sound forth your Joy.

There are no barriers at the centre of your Being, only the flow of energy. Within that flow, listen to the whispers of Wisdom from your friends in other Dimensions who wish to speak to you or through you.

Allow the flow

·

(8TH November 2010)

11

PERSONAL CHOICE

(The circle opens with the Sounds of the Tibetan Bowls and the Crystal Bowl)

Greetings, Dear Hearts, I am Djwahl Khul.

I wish to remind you this evening of the importance of *'personal choice'*. As you look out upon your World at this time, you may notice that in many countries of your World people are exercising *'personal choice'* through elections.

Many of your large countries are going through election processes, each one contributing to the changes that are taking place on the Earth Planet at this time. It is all too easy for you to look upon elections as simply an exercise in 'political choices', but in reality, Dear Ones, each time you cast a vote in an election you are making a *'personal choice'*, you are looking at your perceptions of the world that you want to create, and through the element of what you call politics, you begin to create that new World through the *'personal choices'* that you make.

Vast numbers of people on your Planet at this time are moving through that process, perhaps unnoticed by others outside their own individual countries, but if you are taking a global perspective on the changes that are taking place, you need to be very conscious of the choices that people are making.

There are still, of course, many countries on your Earth where people do not have a choice, they are unable to cast a vote, and in many countries that do have votes to cast, there are many who choose not to do so. They allow changes to be made around them but they do not contribute to those changes by making choices themselves.

As you move into the New Earth frequencies, it is becoming more and more important for each and every individual upon the Planet to exercise the right of *'personal choice'*.

Because in terms of elections, you are creating a change on a country level, you may not necessarily achieve your personal desires because it becomes a collective desire, but that is no reason to withhold your choice. By exercising your choice you paint a little colour into what is achieved by the outcome of your elections.

It is time, Dear Hearts, to look at the World differently, to look at the World as ever changing, to realize the need to express what is within your Heart through the choices you make.

It may seem, Dear Hearts, that this is not a Spiritual message, and many, many people on your Planet hold back thinking that politics are not Spiritual, but in reality politics are the *'community expression' of Spirituality*. It is so easy to sit back and cast judgments, but it is much, much more important, Dear Hearts, to step forward and make choices. Your personal choice should never be taken for granted, and expressing your personal choices is necessary to implement the changes on your Earth Planet. Do you understand what I am saying, Dear Hearts?

Sometimes, Dear Hearts, we sit in Council, in Spiritual Dimensions, and each one of us is required to express our *'personal choices'*. We may not always achieve the dreams we have, the desires we have, but we know that unless we express those dreams and desires, they will never materialize, they will never influence the outcome of decisions that have to be made.

Do you wish to have a World in which you have no input?

Look around the World at this time, at the countries that are going through a process of electing new governments, creating changes of policy. One of your largest countries, India, is going through such a process now. One of your most devastated countries, Afghanistan, is going through those processes now. There are other countries also who are going through this, your own country, Australia, has been through this.

You may not like the outcome, but you know that by expressing your personal feelings, dreams and desires, you are at least contributing to the final outcome. Humanity for eons of time have been content to leave the ruling to a small number of people, and that has not achieved what the world needs to achieve.

Every Heart, every Light upon the Earth needs to be expressed for the whole of the Earth to ascend into Lightness.

If you give away your power to others, how can you complain when things are not the way you wish them to be? In every moment of every day, Dear Hearts, make your own choices and express your own choices, for you are all a part of the ONE.

You all have a unique colour to add to the tapestry of the Earth.

Your *'personal choice'* may not appear to influence the outcome in another country, in another part of the World, but it does, because in making your choice to be Loving, Peaceful and Joyful, you are creating an energy that influences others, you give others permission to express THEIR choices.

So tonight, Dear Hearts, I am simply here to ask you to look around your Earth at this time, to let your Love and your Light flow to those who have been given the opportunity to express their choices - not to seek a specific outcome, but simply to support each and every one of those Beings of Light to take their own power and hold their own Light, and express their own choices.

So be it, Dear Hearts, so be it.

(7th April 2014)

12

WALK THE LABYRINTH OF LOVE

(The Circle opens with the Sounds of the Tibetan Bowls and the Blessings Chimes and the Drum)

Greetings Beloveds, I am Djwahl Khul.

It is interesting that those who will soon be participating in what you refer to as your Olympics are said to be joining the Olympic family, for the energies that are coming to the Earth at this time are very much concerned with family – not family in the limited form that you know it, but family in its greater form.

Many of you are coming into contact with *'soul family'* at this time, coming together to share Unconditional Love in the lead up to the great shift. The energies are also about the greater family of Humanity. This thing you call the Olympics is a wonderful opportunity to focus this energy, for it is a time when, all across your Planet, attention will be focused on one place, at one time.

Although it is the participants who are regarded as being part of the Olympic family, you are all a part of the Olympic family.

As you come closer and closer to this happening, you begin to embrace the rest of the people in your area, in your country, to support your athletes. You become a family within your country.

Although the Olympics may seem to some to be confrontational, pitting one Being against another, it is done within a unique spirit of friendship, of family, of coming together to play out our dreams.

Can you see, Dear Ones, how important moments like these are for your Planet? To have the opportunity to focus these wonderful Cosmic energies through your Heart, and focus them on the one place on Earth that everyone else will be focused on too, radiating Divine Light and Unconditional Love.

You feel part of your family, but you are not a family at war with other families, you are a family coming together with other families.

Those who participate invariably find great Love and great friendship, for they accept each other. They do not judge each other on the basis of their religions, on the basis of the colour of their skins. For just a short time they embrace each other as equals.

Just as the participants do this, so too the opportunity is there for those supporting those participants to come together with others in the same way, sharing Divine Unconditional Love.

There are always many layers to events of this nature, Dear Ones, and you need to look beyond the obvious, you need to look at the opportunities that moments like this present to you, present to the whole of Humanity - the opportunity to come together in Love. Oh yes, there will be competition, but competition within the energy of Love, within the energy of Respect, within the energy of Honour.

Each time these events come around, Humanity is given an opportunity to become the family of Humanity, when you do not look upon the differences of others, but you look upon those aspects that draw you together. The essence of family is Unconditional Love, so the family of the Olympics is an opportunity for each and every one of you to become a part of that family of Love.

On this coming occasion I invite you again to look beyond the obvious, to see within the symbolisms that will be used, the essence of the changes that are taking place within the Earth at this time.

It has already been widely announced that as part of the opening ceremony of the Olympics *(this refers to the London Olympics)* there will be a symbolic Glastonbury Tor. The Glastonbury Tor, as you all know, Dear Ones, is the confluence of the Michael and Mary Lines, the coming together of the Divine masculine and the Divine feminine, which again, Dear Ones, is what the energy which is coming from the Cosmos is all about. It is about coming into Oneness, about embracing the Divine masculine, the Divine feminine within yourselves, and here in the very symbolism of the opening of the Olympic Games will be this projection of the Divine feminine and the Divine masculine.

Of course, Dear Ones, as well you know, the Glastonbury Tor is the physical remainder of the Sacred Isle of Avalon, so the focus right at the opening ceremony will be on this Divine Love energy, so if you, in knowing this, focus your Hearts and project your energy into this representation of the Tor, you build anew the essence of Oneness.

Imagine, Dear Hearts, the power as the focus from around the world is on that one symbol. For just a fleeting moment of your time imagine the in-pouring and the out-pouring of Love through this confluence of the Divine masculine and the Divine feminine, and as you connect your Heart to this, you in turn are drawn into this *"Labyrinth of Love"* that the Tor represents.

I invite you now to place this happening within your Hearts and to see it not only as a sporting contest, but as an opportunity to become the "family of Humanity", and to share once again the Unconditional Love, and to reach out and share your Light, and share your Love.

The timing of the Olympic Games is never an accident Dear Ones; it has particular power at this time in the year 2012. It is time of coming together into Oneness, to focus on becoming a *"family of love".*

As you read, or see, or hear of what is happening at that time, in that place, connect yourself in Love - become an artery of Love - drawing in the beautiful energies that the Cosmos is gifting to the Earth at this time, and focusing that energy in that one place, at that one time, that everyone who is connecting to it may feel the Love and see the Light,

And within their Hearts walk that "Labyrinth of Love".

I bless each and every one of you.

(2nd July 2012)

13

HOLOGRAM OF SHAMBHALA IN YOUR HEART

(The Circle opens with the Sounds of the Tibetan Bowls and the Blessings Chimes)

Greetings Beloved Ones, I am Djwahl Khul, the one you know as the Tibetan.

I come to you this evening to embrace you with the Light of Shambhala. It will indeed soon be the Wesak time. It is important on this occasion to prepare yourselves well for this special occasion, for although Shambhala is indeed a Citadel of Light above the Wesak Valley in Tibet, Shambhala is also a Hologram within the Hearts of each and every one of you.

As your Earth moved into a new Dimensional frequency at the Solstice of December last year, you are now working as Light Workers in two different Dimensions, that of the Third and that of the Fifth. You are anchoring energies into the new Fifth Dimensional frequency, shedding those energies of the Third Dimension that you no longer need or require. Everything upon and within the Earth, and indeed in the surrounding Ethers, are also shifting in frequency. So it is important on this occasion to work most powerfully with the energies of Shambhala in both Dimensional frequencies, to allow the Citadel of Light to flow with ease and grace into its new orbital frequency with the New Earth.

So I am here tonight to ask each and every one of you to move into that Hologram of Light within your Heart that **IS** Shambhala. To connect powerfully and deeply with this meeting place of the Masters, of Guides, of visitors from other Planetary Systems, for in Shambhala all come together as **ONE**, all come together in Peace and Love, and all come together to share their own Light and their own Love with each other. By moving within the Shambhala in your Heart, you will be contributing your Light and your Love to this gathering.

This is the first such gathering since the Earth shifted in frequency. It is still in a parlous state, not yet firmly in balance in its new vibrational frequency. It requires every ounce of Love and Light that you possess to anchor it into its new

Dimensional frequency, to anchor the Shambhala into its new orbital frequency. Open yourselves now to the energies of Shambhala, allow your Heart to expand and embrace the Citadel of Light, and all those within it. Feel yourself drawn powerfully to the many different areas within the Citadel of Light to commune, to embrace, your Spirit friends, the Angels, the Masters, those that are referred to as Aliens on your Planet, but who are Light Beings from other Cosmic Sources, all with a single intent that Love becomes the overwhelming, overpowering, energy of the Earth. From that Love, Peace will flower in a way that Peace has never flowered on this Planet since the beginning of your time.

Take a moment to focus every aspect of your Being, your multi-Dimensional Being, into that Hologram of Light within your Heart – the Shambhala Vibration. Feel it pulse within your Heart with the vibration of Love and Peace. Feel yourself meld with those energies, becoming *ONE* with the Light frequency of Shambhala. Reach out and embrace your friends, look around you, be amazed at how many of the Angels, the Masters, the Guides are friends of yours, Beings that you have spent many lifetimes with,

Beings equal - never smaller or greater - Beings of Light that are in Oneness with you.

At the time of the Wesak in your month of May the ceremonies will be of greater power than ever before. The beloved Buddha energy will expand and flow and connect with the Christed energies, and create new vibrational frequencies of Love and Light upon your Planet, and within your Hearts.

It is time for you, within your own Heart, to prepare the way for this gigantic inflow of Love energy, a time when the Blue Light of Peace will penetrate every pore of the Earth. The Blue Light of Peace will surround and embrace and infuse every Being on the Planet. You will feel, you will notice, and you will know that a greater level of Light has been gifted to the Earth at this time, it is a time of coming into Oneness. Where ever you are, where ever you go in this month of May, you will sow the seeds of Light and you will reap the flower of Light, you will become *ONE*.

So I ask you now to work with the Hologram of Shambhala in your Hearts in every moment of every day, and know that even thought your conscious mind might not be upon that task, you *are* undertaking that task, that the Light quotient of the Planet increases moment by moment, hour by hour, day by day, until the time of the Wesak Ceremony, when the Buddha's energy will **flow**.

It is time to prepare the way, take your time, rest within the Shambhala in your Heart, expand, allow your wisdom to become a part of the pool of Wisdom of All that is.

Let the Harmonics of the Hologram of Shambhala Sound from your Heart, creating the Light through Sound.

Allow your heart to proclaim, *"I AM THE LIGHT OF SHAMBHALA"*, and know that this is so and *ALL ARE ONE*.

And so I leave you Dear Ones.

(3RD May 2010)

14

EQUALITY, EQUALITY, EQUALITY

(The Circle opens with the Sounds of the Tibetan Bowl, the Blessings Chimes and the Drum)

Greetings Beloveds, I am Djwahl Khul, the one you call "The Tibetan"

I come tonight to speak to you of your worth. We, your Spirit friends, do not judge who is more worthy, or who is more important on this journey of Ascension. We accord each of you an equal billing in this grand Play. It is time for each one of you to acknowledge your worth and your participation.

It is all too easy to look at others, to believe that they are contributing more to the process and to the journey than are you yourself, for you never see the true worth of the Light that you radiate and project. Not everything is measured in terms that your minds can understand. Simply by being open of Heart, and by being in your own Light, you each contribute to the whole of your Planet's journey.

You have looked at this one and seen what this one has done (*referring to David's trip to Turkey*) Do not allow that to overwhelm you, to see that his part of the journey is greater than your part of the journey. It is imperative at this time that you each acknowledge yourselves, that you each acknowledge your contribution and your Light, for without your contribution and your Light the whole process of Ascension would be slowed and perhaps even stalled.

So do not hide your Light, do not judge yourself in comparison to others. That is an Earthly trait, it is not something done in the Higher Realms. It is certainly not something done by the creator. *YOU ARE BORN EQUAL.* You may perceive yourself as less equal than others, when your mind comes into play and you begin to make judgements based on a perceived valuation. With your judgements, if you need to make judgements, do so from within your Hearts, and not within your minds. For your minds have been conditioned to a hierarchical structure, and you perceive the efforts of others to be greater than the efforts of yourself. This is not so. *ALL LIGHT HAS EQUAL VALUE*

The Light that is projected from your Heart is equal to the Light projected from another's Heart. It does not matter if you shed your Light upon one person or a thousand persons, your Light is still the same. It still radiates at a constant level, and it provides an integral part of the Ascension process.

Take a moment to enfold yourself within the Light of your own Heart, feel the blessing of that Light, do not look outside yourself, simply embrace yourself with your whole Light, and know deep within your Heart that your Light is unique. There is no other within your Universe who can shed your Light, and your Light is as great as anyone else's. It is so important Dear Ones to remember this. ***YOUR LIGHT IS AS IMPORTANT AS ANYONE ELSE'S.***

You may choose to direct your Light, to set goals, to set achievements of what you wish the energy to do, but when it comes down to it, your Light simply ***IS***. Its place within the whole structure of your Universe simply ***IS. When you close your Hearts, you close off your Light, and part of the Universe dims accordingly.*** No one else can substitute their Light for yours, for yours is unique within the Universe.

Feel the power of your Light within your Heart, embrace it, nurture it, accept its existence, acknowledge your worth.

You have seen, you have read, you have experienced Beings that seem to you to have greater Light than others, you have accorded them worship …Jesus, Mohammed and many many others, but they are simply a *different Light* to yours, no greater, no lesser. Think about that for a moment. Your Light is as important as theirs.

You do not look and count how many people your Light touches, for you do not know this, for you are within your Light, and you radiate it. You do not confine it to other individuals, or even to other situations, you simply contribute your Light to the whole spectrum of Light within your Planet, and within your Universe. *Equality, Equality, Equality.* Once you accept within your Heart that you are equal with all others, and your Light is as important as all others, you begin to grow your Light. Grow it, Develop it. Allow it to shine more and more brightly.

Again, you are not trying to replace the Light of someone else, you are simply *Being* the total Light that you can be, and *that is why you are here Dear*

Ones. You are here to be the most powerful Light that you can be. So open your Hearts and allow that to happen, and do not concern yourself with how far your Light may shine. *It shines where it is meant to shine.*

Your Spirit Friends have often said to you *"We do not know more, we simply know different, for we are unique Lights also"* When these points of Light come together into a whole, the Oneness of all that is begins to emerge. If you withdraw your Light, the Oneness of all that is cannot be complete. So I come to you tonight Dear ones to say, let go of your judgements of yourself and of others, and simply embrace the Light you truly are. *Equal in all measures with all others.*

Blessings be upon you all Dear Ones.

(16th November 2009)

15

'REVISION', DEAR HEARTS, 'REVISION'

(The Circle opens with the Sounds of the Tibetan bowls, the drum and the Tingsha Bells)

Allow the vibrations of the bowls and the drum to enfold you, to create within you a pulsing rhythm that lifts the Love energy within your Heart and sends it forth across the Earth to embrace ALL upon the Planet, to share the most beautiful energy you possess, freely with no expectation of return, gifting the Love within your Hearts, embracing ALL.

Greetings Dear Hearts, I am Djwahl Khul.

I wish to speak to you tonight about **'revision'**. I am sure that many of you will remember that word from your school days when you were coming to the end of your school year and about to sit your examinations, your teacher would say to you "it is important to revise what you have learned in the past year, or in the years before. You need to go back. 'Revision' is the key to passing the test that you are about to take".

How many of you did the **'revision'** ?, how many of you felt it was a 'waste of time'? After all you knew it all, and it is true you know everything that you have experienced in the past, every breath you take, every word you hear, every word you read is stored within your brain. It never leaves you, but it does from time to time become stored in areas of your brain that you never visit again !

Well, Dear Hearts, you are approaching your 'test', for each influx of energy to the Earth Planet from the Cosmos is a 'test', an examination of how well you have absorbed the lessons that have been provided for you in your existence in this lifetime, for without the accumulated knowledge you are unable to properly embrace and access the energies to lift you into the next stage of your journey.

You see a test or an examination is never the 'end point', it is merely a 'staging post' for the next part of your journey, so 'revision' is important.

You have already been told that there will be a new influx of energy coming soon to awaken - to open - the Pyramids of Joy around your Planet, but are you ready to feel the energy of Joy? You have been prepared over the past years for the inflow of this energy, but it is time now to take a moment or two for **'revision'**, for looking back at the events, the information, that has come to you over recent times, over the past 12 months, the past few years, and to draw from that information that which is necessary in order for you to pass the next test, to move onto the next stage of your journey - the stage that is filled with the energy of Joy.

You have been told many times, "let go of the past", but what that has meant, Dear Ones, is to let go of those aspects of your past which are no longer relevant to the New Earth Energies, to the new you within the New Earth Energies.

So you do not press 'delete' on your past and remove everything, you simply 'revise', you look at all that has happened and you bring forward into your 'examination' that which will empower you, that which will allow you to embrace the new energies of Joy.

Joy can be an overpowering energy, so it is important to put in place the foundations to enable you to cope with and embrace these powerful energies. So tonight I call upon you, I remind you of *'revision'*, for some of you that may mean simply reflecting on your past, for others it may be *'revisiting'* some of the messages that you have received from your Spiritual friends over the past 12 months.

Because Humanity operates within linear time, it is all too easy to forget what happened yesterday. It has no relevance your mind tells you, it is gone, and yet it is part of the fabric of your Being. All knowledge is part of the fabric of your Being, part of the totality of YOU.

The secret of Ascension Dear Hearts, is to know which parts of the information you have gathered over your lifetime is relevant, and important, and necessary for the next stage of your journey.

Each message that is brought to you by your Spiritual friends in your weekly gathering is not necessarily relevant to all of you, but somewhere within those messages there is something for each of you. It is a question, Dear Hearts, of *'revision'*, of looking back and bringing forwards into your minds now, the hints, the tips, the knowledge, the wisdom that has been imparted, but only those that are relevant to you and your journey. *Discernment as always, Dear Hearts.*

You may for example wish to revisit the 8th and final Labyrinth of your Marine Meditation, perhaps I can remind you - that Labyrinth allowed you to journey within yourself from the fifth to the ninth Dimension of your Soul, but in walking the Labyrinth you are merely creating an energy footprint for the future, so perhaps for some of you it may be important to revisit that Labyrinth and to walk again from the 5th to the 9th Dimension of your Soul, and to feel the energies of each stage of the journey from the Peace in the Heart, to the Awakening.

Powerful, powerful energies, not necessarily relevant to all of you, perhaps only to one of you, but it is an example of something that has happened in your past which you have now left behind.

So, Dear Hearts, *'revision'*. It is time now for *'revision'* in preparation for the next inflow of powerful energies, the energies of Joy.

Take some time to look within yourself and find the *'pearls of wisdom'* that resonate with you. You will know deep within your Being which ones are important for your journey, and which ones you can leave behind.

It is time for your next 'test' and 'examination', a purely personal one for each of you as you move along your Journey of Ascension.

'Revision', Dear Hearts, 'Revision'.

(4th November 2013)

16

ENLIGHTENMENT AND ILLUMINATION

(The Circle opens with the Sounds of the Tibetan bowls and the Crystal bowl)

Feel the Sound vibrations releasing all the tensions within your physical vessel, allowing for the free flow of energy, the free flow of Light through every aspect of your Being. *Feel the upliftment.* Feel the essence of Joy within your Heart pulsate with the Sound vibration, creating a new energy of unity and oneness.

Greetings Beloveds, I am Djwahl Khul.

I wish to address tonight the subject of *Enlightenment and Illumination*. As has been mentioned on previous occasions, you will shortly be walking your *Labyrinth of Inner Vision*, and moving through the *Portal of Enlightenment and Illumination*.

It is important, Dear Ones, that you do not perceive this as some kind of instant happening. The Portal is merely a doorway to a Dimensional frequency where Enlightenment is possible.

We are well aware in your Dimension that Humanity loves to perceive these occasions as times of miraculous happenings, and are so frequently disappointed, when, in their minds, nothing seems to change.

I come to remind you of the words of Beloved Spirit of Crystals and Gemstones – *"Enlightenment can only occur when Wisdom is aligned with Understanding".*

The Earth has been suffused by the energies of understanding at the 11.11.11, and in the time since the 11.11.11, for the attainment of Enlightenment is a gradual process. In Human terminology you could say it is a "joining up of the dots", creating new perceptions and new perspectives on the wisdom that you have already attained through your many lifetimes. We speak often about "living in the now", but unfortunately Humanity sometimes takes this to mean that you should forget what has gone before, and perhaps not even dream of what is to come, but that is not so.

The attainment of Enlightenment is an accumulative process. You will have noticed over the last few weeks of your time, that we have raised to your awareness again *"pearls of wisdom"* that were gifted to you decades ago, that have been lying dormant within you, and are now raised to your awareness once again, so that you may look upon them with a new understanding, a new Enlightenment.

We have raised with you the question of allowing the flow of energy when you are considering protection. We have also raised with you the need to look at your life through your Heart.

These have all been raised with you before. Part of what you do now - between this time and the walking of the Portal of Enlightenment - is to bring to your awareness all that wisdom that you have accumulated, for you will need this wisdom, you will need to share this wisdom with those around you who are just beginning to awaken.

You have all served the Earth in many ways, in many lifetimes, and *you are a library of wisdom, but Wisdom without Understanding has no meaning*. We seek therefore to bring together the two aspects – the Wisdom and the Understanding - that you may attain the necessary Enlightenment for you to become truly the Light Bearers in the new Earth frequency. That you may embrace your fellow Humans with your Wisdom, with your Understanding, and create a *Oneness of Enlightenment.*

I am sure you understand what I am speaking of – the time for people, Humans, to use the Wisdom they have been given to dominate others, is over. This is a time of sharing - sharing your Wisdom - sharing your Understanding - sharing your Light.

In order to do this, Dear Ones, you must first understand yourself. You must first understand that what you put out for others to see, is what you will receive back from them.

Another aspect of wisdom that has been given to you previously, there was much to-do a number of years ago about the *"Secret".* There is no Secret – there is only the Law of Attraction - *what you put out, you receive back - amplified.*

It is imperative, in this year in particular, with the energies that are flooding into the Earth at this time, amplifying the changes that are taking place, that you are conscious of what you are putting out into the world.

It is not about being wiser or better than others. It is simply about <u>being your Light</u>, and allowing others to share that Light.

Tonight I give you another *"pearl of wisdom"* that has been gifted to you many times before –

*"Project yourself
from the Light within your Heart,
not the shadows within your mind".*

Think on that a moment, Dear Ones. In whatever you do, and where ever you go in the coming times, project yourself from the Light within your Hearts, not the shadows within your mind.

For as people see and feel the Light energy radiating from you, they will be calmed, and they will feel Love. They may not initially understand what they are feeling, but they will be moved and changed by the energies that you are radiating. You are not sharing your Light in order to dominate others. You are simply sharing your Light because that is what is within your Heart.

As you move forward on your journey, focus always on your Heart.

Change invariably creates discomfort and doubts, and these are what is referred to as the "shadows of your mind". Indeed, you have an expression on your Planet when someone is certain, you say - "without a shadow of doubt".

Now, Dear Ones we are asking you to let go of these "shadows of doubt", and to know with complete certainty that *the Light within your Hearts is the guidance for the whole of Humanity.*

From time to time as the year goes on, we may remind you of more of the wisdom that has been given to you in past times, that you may look afresh and share anew that which you already know.

I leave you now with a blessing from the Light from within **My** Heart -

> *Be one*
> *Be always within your Heart*

I bless you.

And so it is.

(9th January 2012)

17

MOVING FROM LIGHT BEARER TO LIGHT GIVER

(The Circle opens with the Sounds of the Tibetan Bowls, the Blessings Chimes and the Drum)

Feel yourselves being totally uplifted by the Blessings Chimes, allowing the energies of Blessing to fill your Being with Light Frequencies that dance across the Universe, and across the Earth, and through every atom of your Being, for you are here upon the Earth to be a Blessing for all you meet.

This has nothing to do with your persona as a Human, it has to do with your *VIBRATION*. When you allow Love to flow from deep within your Heart, you create a vibration of Light that cascades from you and embraces all around you, all those of the Human race, but also ALL upon the Earth and the Earth itself.

Acknowledge and accept the brilliance of your own Light and empower it with every breath you take, for it is your Light, that is the contribution you make to the Ascension of the Earth Planet, it is not your wisdom or your wit but your *Light,* your *Colour,* your *Sound.*

Greetings Dear Hearts, I am Dwahl Khul.

It is a great privilege for me to join you after such a powerful Equinox, a time of great Joy and a time of great change. Gateways have been opened to other Dimensional Frequencies and there will be many upon your Earth that will choose to walk through those gateways, to transcend their Earth journey and to become *'Lights in the Universe'*, and there will be many more who will choose to walk through those gateways onto the Earth Planet to bring their unique Light to bear on the Ascension process that your world is moving through at this time.

Many of you here in this Circle have worked for many lifetimes to reach this point of reconnection with your universal heritage. *You have come to this Planet to be a Blessing FOR this Planet and you have ALL achieved this.* You may not see the impact that as an individual you have upon the Light of the Earth itself, but let me assure you, Dear Hearts, each contribution is magnificent and profound, and together you create the Oneness of all that is.

The Equinox you have just witnessed was particularly powerful with a solar eclipse and new moon and many other Planetary alignments, all that came together to create an explosion of Light that has radiate far out into the Universe and sent messages of Love to all your Home Planets.

Now is the start of new journeys for each and every one of you, and your Spirit friends will be there to walk alongside you, to assist you as you move forward with your new contracts to the Earth, and your new contracts to the Universe and the Omniverse.

There are no ends, only new beginnings, and there is no going back into the darkness of the past. You may look around you at areas of your Planet that are in turmoil at this time and wonder where the Light is, well Dear Hearts, ***the Light is within YOU, but it is not in you to remain in you, it is in you to be gifted to the Earth.***

This is a new time of Love, a new time of passion for all that is the Earth, the Oceans and the Land.

Gradually from this time on there will be a new relationship between Humanity and the Earth upon which they walk, one that is based on *respect and caring and Love.*

There will be new and wonderful inventions that will help to create this bonding afresh between Humanity and the Earth, and each and every one of you will have a part to play, and each will be as important as the next.

So let go of all feelings of lack or inadequacy and fully embrace the Love and the Light within your Heart, and shine it forth with determination, with commitment - *moving from a LIGHT BEARER to a LIGHT GIVER.*

Feel the Joy and the Love flowing around this Circle at this moment, feel it uplifting you, feel it infusing you, feel it bringing a smile to your faces as you look ahead and see the New Earth rising up within each Being, finding the Colour and the Sound and the Light within you, and sending that deep into the Earth, for this is a new journey for each and every one of you - *the journey into your Heart and beyond.*

(23rd March 2015)

18

IT IS TIME TO PARTY !!!!!

(The gathering opens with the Sounds of the Tibetan Bowl, the Drum and the Peace and Harmony Chime)

Greetings, Dear Hearts, I am Djwahl Khul, and it is a great delight to be with you once more in the Pendragon Sacred Space, it has been a considerable time since we have shared these moments of Oneness together, but much has been happening upon the Earth Planet and beyond the Earth Planet.

It would be very easy for each one of you to be filled with fear, but I am here to say there is no need for fear, ALL IS AS IT IS MEANT TO BE. When great changes take place upon a Planet there is a time of turmoil, and people begin to feel fear, but I ask you, Dear Hearts, to move deep within yourselves and find the stillness that is at the Heart of your Being, and in that stillness you will find *PEACE,* and as you allow that Peace to grow within you, you begin to radiate it forth out into your world, to replace the fear, to bring a new sense of *JOY* to all life upon the Earth Planet.

Over this last period of time, Dear Hearts, as you well know, much effort has been made to seed a new Arcturian Peace Energy into the Crystalline Grids of the Earth by Beloved Tarak and Margot, and I am delighted to say they have been most successful in their endeavors. It has not been without its problems, of course, for there is a great deal of fear and turmoil upon your Planet at this time, and they have needed to cut through this veil of fear, and to seed the new Peace Energies into the Earth. This will be completed at the time of your next Equinox, so I am here to call upon you, Dear Hearts, to work with Beloved Tarak and Margot upon that particular day, to focus your attention on them and on the Crystalline Grid structure of the Earth – both those that are visible, and those that are invisible beneath the oceans of your world – and to join with them in celebration of this monumental event.

Dear Hearts, when you create a structure upon your Planet it is customary, is it not, to have an 'unveiling' Ceremony, to have a Party, a celebration of an achievement, and this is what we are inviting you to do upon your Equinox this time. Let go of all your worries, all your fears, and set aside some time upon that day to *be Joyful*, to *Have a party!* for this is indeed the beginning, and not the end of the process of creating a *Planet of Peace.*

You see, Dear Hearts, it is not the role of those in the Spirit World, those in the Cosmic Realms to create Peace upon the Earth Planet, that, Dear Hearts, is your role ! all that can be done by others is to create the circumstances under which *Peace can be created by you.*

Imagine it, if you will, Dear Hearts, as a farm. When a farmer wishes to create crops to feed the world, first he needs to prepare the soil, to give the best possible opportunity for the seeds he plants to grow into the fruits of his labor. This is what Beloved Tarak and Margot have been doing, Dear Hearts, they have been preparing the Earth, bringing sufficient nutrients into the Earth Planet to enable the seeds of Peace that you then plant to come to fruition. It is a joint venture, Dear Hearts, there is no point in you sitting upon your seats and thinking *'someone else will create Peace for me and I just need to embrace it'.* **NO**, Dear Hearts, we have told you many times before, Peace begins deep within the Hearts of each individual. It is for them, it is for you, to allow that Peace to radiate forth from your Being and to join with the Peace that others are radiating forth until it reaches a 'critical mass' and becomes the dominant force upon your Earth Planet.

There is no one single solution to the problems of the Earth Planet, it is about coming together in Oneness about creating *Communities of Peace*.

Peace does not *Fight* ! Dear Hearts, *Peace* simply *Exists,* and permeates the atmosphere, and then permeates every Being upon the Planet and gradually they begin to change their ways, to change the way they think, the way they feel. We are here to support you in every way we can, but we are not here to do it for you, Dear Hearts, this is *Your Journey* !

At times you may feel that it is all too much, all too difficult, there are those in power who have more power, no, Dear Hearts ! no one, no one at all has power over you – unless you allow them to have that power.

The new Arcturian Peace Energy that has been seeded into the Crystalline Grid structure of the

Earth Planet allows you to plant the seeds of *Peace* from within your own Hearts and to tend those seeds by sharing as much *Love* and *Joy* with others as you can. Yes there are times you are able to sit back and watch this grow, watch others around you start to awaken to the Light and the Love within themselves, and then you embrace them with your Light. You hold out the hands of friendship, of Love, of commitment to Oneness, and *everything changes once more.* Shadows will fade as the sun reaches its zenith - that sun, Dear Hearts, is the Peace within your Heart.

And so, Dear Hearts, as you move towards your Equinox think about the preparations that have already been made, the Earth is now receptive, filled with Nutrients of Love waiting for you to plant your seeds. So, at your Equinox focus your attention, focus your Hearts on the new Peace Energies. In Particular, Dear Hearts, if you do need a particular focus, then I ask you to focus upon Mt. Kailash, for it is through Mt, Kailash that the *CONSCIOUSNESS* of this Peace has flowed through to the Earth. So focus upon Mt, Kailash, allow the Consciousness of Peace to fill you, and embrace the Crystalline Grids of the Earth. Embrace the Songlines of the

Earth, become **ONE** with them, and as you do, feel the energy of Joy start to emerge from where it has been hiding for so long within you.

MOVE INWARDS IN ORDER TO MOVE OUTWARDS ! rather than move outwards in order to move inwards ! This is the great change that is about to take place, Dear Hearts, it is about no longer reaching outwards but reaching inwards, for everything you need, all the Love, all the Peace, all the Joy, is already within you.

You have been hiding it from the World, now, now is the time to reveal to all of Humanity the Love, the Peace and the Joy that you have been holding within you for your whole lifetime, your many lifetimes, for the Earth itself has changed and it is inviting you to change, to become the Light Beings you really are, to transcend the physicality of the Earth System and become once more Light, Love, Joy and Peace.

Dear Hearts, at your Equinox, **IT IS TIME TO PARTY !!!!!** We look forward to sharing that Joyful day with you, and to contribute our Peace, our Love and our Joy, and do not forget those who are non Human upon your Planet, particularly the Whales and the Dolphins who have 'held in balance' your

Earth Planet for so long, embrace them, embrace the Oceans of your World for they reflect the 'emotions' of your World, at the moment they are turbulent, Dear Hearts, in many parts of your world, this is the final change, that is taking place, They are ready !!

ARE YOU READY ??????

Blessings, Dear Hearts, we will all be partying with you.

(11th September 2017)

19

11:11:11

(The Circle opens with the Sounds of the Tibetan Bowls and the Blessings Chimes and the Drum)

Very powerful messages have just been read, each of which was designed to ensure that you realize your own part in what is happening on the Earth at this time - the importance of your own Light and Life - the importance of accepting the responsibility of allowing that Light to shine forth, to assist all those who are yet to awaken to the Light within themselves.

(The Tibetan Bowls Sound.)

Greetings Beloveds, I am Djwahl Khul, and I thank you for allowing me to embrace the powerful and beautiful energy of this Circle this evening. Much is being written and spoken of the upcoming 11:11:11, so much so, that there is a danger of Humanity falling back into the old paradigm of perceiving this momentous occasion as something external to themselves.

There are many stories of what will happen at this time, but all that will happen is what you create within your own Hearts.

There is no significant event that will transpire sourced from outside of your own Hearts.

It is important Dear Ones to maintain your perceptions of Unity, of Oneness. The Crystalline Grid Systems of the Earth have already become ONE.

What the 11:11:11 does, is create the possibilities, create a focus for your Heart to create with the influx of energies from the Cosmos, the Earth that you have dreamed of for eons of time. I repeat that Dear Ones – "create what you have wanted for eons for time".

The number 11 has a resonance of Transformation, as such it is a powerful "after quake" from the Equinox when you walked your *Portal of Transformation,* and moved from the Realm of Separateness, into the Realm of Unity.

The significance of a trinity of 11 numbers substantially increases the inflow of energy to the Earth at this time, but energy has no purpose until it is taken within your Heart and focused into specific intent.

This is why Dear Ones, you, I repeat - you - will create with the energies that are flowing into the Earth. The 11:11:11 will simply provide an opportunity and a focus for you to do this. Each gathering around your Planet will have a different focus. No one focus is greater than another. All will come together into the whole through the Divine Love within your own Hearts.

There is a certain illusion involved in the 11:11:11, for humanity conveniently ignores the fact that there is also a number 2 involved.

The reality is that it is 11:11:2011, and when each 11 is reduced to its smallest component, it too becomes a 2. So in effect you have a 2:2:2:2, which I am sure you will all know comes to an 8.

8 is the power number of this Circle - it is infinite, eternity, so it offers the opportunity once more to create the Eternal Love, the Eternal Light, to transform our Planet through the Light and Love within our own Hearts.

Each of you will be directed according to what is within your own Hearts - not the visions and dreams of others - purely and simply what is within your own Heart.

What is your vision for the future of the Earth? Do not think that you all have to have the same visions, Dear Ones, the Creator is not singular. It is omnipresent. There is room for many visions, providing each comes from the energy of Divine Love within the Hearts of each Being.

So focus not on what is the vision of others, what are the beliefs of others - focus on the Love and the Light within your own Hearts, and see the Earth as you would like it to be.

There will undoubtedly be similarities in the visions - you will all no doubt want a World of Peace, a World of Love, a World of Respect and Understanding. The more that focus on this, the greater the possibility of the Earth becoming that vision.

Within the ONE, there is the many, so allow your own Light to create your own vision and add it to the whole.

Some perceive the 11:11:11 as an opportunity to reawaken the past, the times of Atlantis, and Lemuria, and the energies of those times are indeed important and powerful aspects of what is to come. Do not feel that these are the only opportunities on which to focus.

Embrace the Light of *ALL*, but most of all focus your own Light, from your own Heart, and *dream your dream of the Earth you wish to be.*

That is why you have come here at this time, because your Light, your Love, your Dream is important to the future of your Planet.

We too, in the Realms of the Ascended Masters, We have our Dreams, We have our Light, We have our Love, and We will join them with Yours.

We will not overtake your dreams, we will embrace them, and we will create with you a new Earth of immense Love, and immense Light.

Blessings be upon each and every one of you.

We look forward to sharing the 11:11:11 and the 2:2:2:2.

And so it is.

(24th October 2011)

20

COSMIC SYMPHONY
OF DIVINE LOVE

(The Circle opens with the Sounds of the Tibetan Bowl and the Blessings Chimes)

Listen to the Sound of Love deep within your Hearts. Simply open your Being and listen to this Sound Vibration with every atom of your Being, for the Sound of Love within your own Heart goes well beyond the frequencies that your human ear can detect.

The Sound of Divine Love is all encompassing, it embraces all frequencies, all Harmonic notes. It is the Music of the Cosmos. Allow yourself to simply listen to the Sound of Love.

As you listen, feel your whole Being becoming Harmonised and Enlightened, lifting you up, expanding you out, becoming the true Multidimensional Being that you are.

Listen to the Sound of Divine Love within your Heart. The vibration of your Love connects and interacts with all the vibrations of Divine Love from all the Beings on this Planet, and from the Earth itself.

You are part of a Cosmic Symphony of Divine Love.

You are a unique note within that Symphony, without you there is no completion of the Symphony. Recognize in that the importance that you hold at this time, at all of time. Your individual note/Tone is of immense importance to the whole.

So as you listen to the Sound of Divine Love from within your own Heart, Honour that Sound. Do not draw it back and feel that it is inferior to the Sound of anyone else, know it is integral to the whole Harmonic Symphony of the Cosmos, for Love is an energy, Love is a frequency. It is both Light and Sound. It is a force of creation.

As you recognize the importance of your note within the Symphony, accord honour and respect to all the other notes. Regard them all as Equals. *There is no greater or smaller, there is only the equality within the Symphony.*

The time has come when the Light and the Love within yourself becomes your guidance. *Trust that which is within yourself.*

In times of great change, times that the Earth is moving through now, there will always be those in fear who seek to diminish your Light because of their own fear. So trust totally in what is within you. *Do not take on board the fears expressed by others.*

When you are given anything which seeks to diminish your Light, *LET IT GO !!* embrace only that which is empowering to your Light. That, Dear Heart, is your definition of Truth.

Energies that uplift and enhance you, and support your trust in yourself – those are your Truth. Let anything other than that fade away. Do not focus on it, do not give it your Light – let it fade away.

The importance now, Dear Ones, is
   To accept your Divinity,
   To flow with your Divinity,

To recognize your part in the great Symphony of the Cosmos, and

To honour all those who support your Divine Love.

Listen closely to the Sound of the Divine Love within your Hearts, and feel your Light increasing in its power, in its brightness, in its brilliance.

It is time to awaken and believe in your own Divinity.

I am Djwahl Khul, and I bless you my children, and I bless you with Light, and with the Sound of my Love.

(21ST February 2011)

21

THE AWAKENING OF HUMANITY TO COMMUNITY

(Tibetan Bowls were Sounded)

Allow the Sound and the harmonics of the Tibetan bowls, to resonate deep within your Being, calling out a message of Oneness, of Unity, of Wholeness, deep within yourself.

Each individual note is part of a Cosmic Melody - a Melody of Love. Feel it resonating through every aspect of your Being, drawing everything within yourself into a harmonious state of Oneness.

Greetings Beloveds, this is Djwahl Khul.

I come tonight to speak to you of the discernment that is necessary at this time of great change.

You are continuing to be presented, through your media with visions of chaos. Allow yourself to observe - but not embrace - these energies of seeming chaos. For what you are seeing is but an illusion - for in those moments of chaos, if you are discerning, you will perceive the energies of Oneness and Unity.

I draw your attention to the recent events in the UK, when chaos upon the streets became a catalyst for the coming together of Community. You needed to see vision of the chaos in order to fully appreciate the energies of Community.

Community is about coming together in Unity for a greater purpose, and you are now seeing evidence of that emerging from the chaos of the days and the weeks before.

You are being shown quite clearly Dear Ones, that to allow yourself to be drawn into the chaos prevents you from seeing the greater picture – the awakening of Humanity to Community.

The people of UNITY were dubbed "The Broom Brigade", were they not?.

This was no different to the natural disasters that you saw previously in your country (*Australia*), and the aftermath, when complete strangers came together in Community to help one another.

So do not allow yourselves to be drawn emotionally into the chaos, but give your energies of Love, to spark the beginning of the energies of Community.

What you are seeing in the World is a reflection of what is happening within yourself. Each of you is moving through periods of chaos in order to appreciate the energies of Community within yourself, bringing all aspects of your Being into alignment, into Oneness.

Discernment, Dear Ones, is of great importance at this time. Look beyond. Look at the biggest picture of all.

Feel the energies of Love, of Peace, of Harmony within your own Being, and then radiate those energies out into the World, choosing to acknowledge that chaos precedes Unity - it awakens souls that are sleeping on the Earth at this time. It is the earthquake within Humanity, shaking it up, allowing it to make judgements about itself, and then move into Love of itself, creating greater respect within oneself, and then sharing that with others.

You will see much more of what you call chaos, so I ask you now to look with the eyes of your

Heart, to look through the eyes of Love, to see with your Inner Vision, the greater picture, the greater picture of the ascension of the Earth and all upon it.

(The Tibetan bowls Sound again)
Embrace the Harmony of Sound, and allow that Harmony of Sound to radiate forth as the Light of Love, embracing the Earth, embracing the Universe.

Embrace the wisdom of your Guides and Spirit Friends, and share *their* wisdom and *your* wisdom at every opportunity.

We are all one.

And so it is.

(15ᵗʰ August, 2011)

22

MAGNETICS ARE A FORM OF COMMUNICATION WITH THE EARTH

(The Circle opens with the Sound of the Tibetan Bowl, the Blessings Chimes and the Drum)

Greetings Dear Hearts, I am Djwahl Khul.

A short time ago we indicated to you that in this new Dimension of Oneness you will be working with *all* your senses, and not just those senses that you have been working with in the old Dimension of separation and duality.

Throughout that time you have comfortably worked with the Physical Dimension, the Emotion Dimension, the Mental Dimension, and the Spiritual Dimension, but you have not worked, for eons of time, with an equally important Dimension - the Dimension of Magnetics.

Humanity has retained the *'knowing'* that the Earth Planet itself is surrounded by a Magnetic field.

Some refer to it as a grid, a Magnetic grid, but what Humanity has chosen to forget is that each and every life form upon the Earth Planet also has a Magnetic field, and there is constant interaction between these Magnetic fields of the individual Light force and the Magnetic field of the Earth.

In the earliest of times Humanity worked with the Magnetics within themselves, and communicated through these Magnetics, with the Magnetics of the Earth. That is why, Dear Hearts, you were almost exclusively nomadic, for you were drawn by the calling of the Earth's Magnetic field to move from place to place, just as the winged ones of the moment are constantly moving, sometimes vast distances across the Earth Planet, because they are called by the Magnetics of the Earth, and it is through their connection with the Magnetics of the Earth that they can move from place to place with total accuracy.

The Light Beings within your Oceans do likewise, they are guided in their journeys, no, indeed, they are called on their journeys by the Magnetics of the Earth, speaking to the Magnetics of themselves.

So what happened to Humanity that did not happen to the winged ones, or those creatures within the

Oceans? The answer is quite simple, Dear Hearts, Humanity determined that they would follow the course of the Mental Body, and instead of accepting the unknown pull of the Magnetics of the Earth, they sought to give this logic, they sought to come together, to gather together, to stop their wandering - and as the mind grew stronger, the Magnetic field was forgotten.

But in the Dimension of Oneness, Dear Hearts, it is important once more for all Beings of Light upon the Earth Planet to once again activate and connect to the Magnetics of themselves.

Whilst we speak of a Magnetic field, or Magnetic grids, they are not constant, they are more a mix of *'oscillating spirals of energy'*, some transmitting and some receiving, and although your minds have chosen to forget the existence of the Magnetics within yourself, they have not ceased to exist.

I have come tonight to alert you to the existence of the Magnetic field of your own Being, and to ask you once again to begin to communicate with your Earth Planet through these Magnetics. Indeed, these are being strengthened daily by an infusion of energy from the Cosmos that over recent times has focused purely on the Magnetics of the Earth and the Magnetics of all upon the Earth.

Part of your Ascension process has been letting go of the power of your mind and releasing it to the power of your Heart, and once you begin to do this, you also open yourself to the power of the Magnetics within yourself.

The Magnetics are a form of communication with the Earth, and of course with the Cosmos, a connection and a communication that bypasses the mind and works entirely with your Heart.

Do not try to think too deeply about how the Magnetic field looks or feels or senses, just allow it to happen, to embrace one more of the powerful senses that Beings of Light possess, and by accepting the existence of the Magnetics and working with them, you will increase the Light quotient within yourself, for you will have let go of another veil, another blockage from the past.

In the Dimension of Oneness you are encouraged to find the wholeness of yourselves, open to the powerful energies from the Cosmos that are flowing into the Earth Planet at this time, empowering the

Magnetics of the Earth and the Magnetics of you, and you will find your relationship to each other, and to the Earth itself will change in dramatic ways - not in ways your mind will see, perceive or understand necessarily, but then your awareness of all things now is not contained within your mind, it is contained within your total Being.

Focus on opening yourself to the magnificence of your own Magnetic Being, and allow that to shed more Light upon your journey.

I bless and embrace your Magnetic Beings.

(10th June 2013)

23

UNIVERSAL SONG OF LIGHT

(The Circle opens with the Sounds of the Tibetan Bowls and the Blessing Chimes.)

Feel yourselves being uplifted into your Soul Dimension. Imagine yourself sitting high above the Earth Planet on a wispy cloud and looking down upon the Earth and seeing the lights of your cities and the darkened areas between the lights of your cities, and radiate forth the Light from within your own Heart to encompass both the lighted areas of the Earth and the darkened areas of the Earth, for there is no separation anymore, the Earth is in ONENESS and is filled with Light even though that Light may not be visible to your eyes - but it is a knowing within your Heart.

The *'Universal Song of Light'* has been embraced by Earth Mother and flows powerfully through the Crystalline Grids and the Song Lines of the Earth, so there is no part of the Earth now that is without Light.

Focus the Love from within your Heart and embrace the whole of the Earth with that Love, setting aside all judgments, all perceptions of right or wrong, but focusing purely on Love and Light, for in the new *'Oneness of Light'* the energies of Peace will begin to grow and spread through every living, breathing Being upon the Earth and throughout the Crystalline Grid System of the Earth and the Magnetic System of the Earth.

You are at the beginning of a new journey of Light - it is not a journey that will be swift, it will be slow, it will be gentle and it will be loving and as you sit upon your cloud in your Soul Dimension and radiate your Love and your Light, know that you are creating a new world, creating a new Star in the Cosmos, and simply allow yourself to BE in that state of Love.

Greetings, Dear Hearts, I am Djwahl Khul.

The energies of the Equinox were profound indeed and much has been brought to the surface of the Earth that has been hidden for so long, pods of Light Beings of many Dimensional frequencies and many civilizations have begun to awaken and contribute the Purity of their Love to the Ascension of Earth Mother.

The new journey has begun and this time, Dear Hearts, there is no turning back, for Earth Mother has now accepted her own Divinity and embraced all upon and within the Earth with that new sense of Divinity. That new *'belief in self'* will empower all Light Beings upon the Earth and will shine Light into all parts of the Earth. ***No one will be able to hide from the Light.***

For a little while after the Equinox a rebalancing will occur within the Earth and within each Being of Light upon the Earth, so do not worry if you are unable immediately to see the new directions of your life. The changes will be slow and gentle and graceful for the Purity of the Love that the new *'Universal Song of Light'* has brought to the Earth is gentleness personified.

So, Dear Hearts, allow yourselves to go with the flow and listen to the promptings of your own Heart and your own knowingness. Too often in the past you have allowed your minds to set aside your intuitions, to set aside your knowingness, to make judgments, but that needs to come to an end. You will be surprised, Dear Hearts, when subtle nudgings of your own Heart become apparent to you – *Follow those Images, those Nudgings, Those Knowings.*

Do not hesitate, do not set them aside for fear of what others may think or feel, it is time now to step forward in your own Light and to have belief in yourselves, and listen also, Dear Hearts, to the promptings of Earth Mother, she will seek to guide you with Love and Light.

Open your Hearts, allow HER LOVE to fill your Heart.

There is a greater togetherness that will emerge upon the Earth, and many of you will be in the front row of this emerging Light and emerging Love, if you *follow the longing within you - the longing of fulfillment, the knowing of Pure Love.*

Spend as much time as you can, Dear Hearts, floating on your cloud in your Soul Dimension, for this is where your promptings will have greater clarity and greater understanding, but remember, Dear Hearts, always act upon the promptings of your own Heart, for when you do so you contribute to the Ascension of the whole. You may not even understand the rationale of what the promptings are asking you to do but that no longer matters, Dear Hearts, *all that matters is that you listen and act when the promptings occur.*

(28th March 2016)

24

CHANGE IS ABOUT ENERGY

(The Circle opens with the Sounds of the Tibetan Bowls and the Drum)

Greetings, Dear Hearts, I am Djwahl Khul, and I embrace you totally and completely with deepest Love, for it is to your Hearts that we continue to speak, and it is within your Hearts that you need to begin to perceive the world around you.

It is so easy, Dear Ones, to speak of changes taking place on your Planet, but if you perceive these changes purely from within the stand point of your mind, you will simply continue the illusion of your separateness.

There is always more to change than the mind can perceive, for *change is about energy, and energy is a thing of the Heart.*

You see the tip of the iceberg when your mind perceives what is happening on your Planet. It is time to move within your Hearts and to look at those changes through the energy within your Hearts, to open yourself to the potential changes, the possibilities that the energy creates.

It is so easy to look at a situation where one person replaces another, and see only the person, but if you move into your Hearts and look again, you see a change of energy, and as you connect to that change of energy you start to create the changes within yourself, changes that you may not be able to give names to, Dear Ones, for names are things of the mind, but changes, subtle changes of energy that you feel, that you sense and that you know deep within your Heart, and you embrace those changes of energy without judgement.

So even when the mind perceives only the change of person and makes judgements according to that, allow your Heart to simply embrace the change of energy, for you will realize, Dear Ones, that in this dimension of Oneness, you are part of that change, you are part of the greater iceberg, of which your mind perceives the tip.

Yes, Dear Hearts, it is so, a change has been made at the top of two of your major religious institutions, but I ask you not to look at the people that have changed, but instead to move into your Heart and embrace the 'energy' that has changed.

Make no judgement, just embrace the energy of change - for you will create influence on that change by accepting it into your own Heart and by filling that energy with Love, and then radiating it out, so that the person who is at the tip of this iceberg is imbued with the collective Unity 'energy' of Humanity, and uplifted far beyond their own perception of their selves.

So many changes will take place in the coming times. Open your Heart and embrace the changes, perceive them and work with them through the energy of Unity and Oneness, know that you are not separate from those changes, even though your mind may perceive you as separate because you are in a different part of the Earth. Perhaps you are part of a different religion. It does not matter, for it is the *'energy'* that is changing. There is more Light, there is more Love, there is more compassion permeating every facet of Human existence, and you can encourage these changes by embracing them, by accepting your Oneness with them, and by focusing, not on judging outcomes, but simply by accepting that each day and each moment of each day, the quotient of Light and Love upon and within the Earth is growing, and growing, and growing.

You have probably noticed within yourselves the changes in your energy, changes in your perceptions of the energies around you. Do not be fearful, do not seek to judge them, do not even seek to understand them necessarily, Dear Ones. Focus on the Love within your Hearts, for as you do so you focus upon the Love within the whole of Humanity. Do not withhold your Love from any Being of Light upon the Earth and within the Earth. *As you empower yourself with Love, you empower the whole of the Earth with Love, and you create magical possibilities.*

Let go of the limitations of your own desires, as they are perceived within your minds, and instead embrace the desires of Oneness within your Heart, and feel the energies of Joy, and the energies of Peace growing within you, moment by moment, and as you look out upon the Earth see everything through the energies of Love, that the Earth itself may vibrate with the energies of Peace, the energies of Oneness, the energies of Love.

I greet you and I bless you, and I thank you for all the work that you have been doing upon your selves, for the Earth, for Humanity.

You are all True Light Beings.

(25th March 2013)

25

WHAT'S NEXT ?

(The Circle opens with the Sounds of the Tibetan Bowls and the Blessings Chimes)

Greetings, Dear Hearts, I am Djwahl Khul.

You were not expecting me to come in so quickly, but the energies within this circle tonight are so beautiful I could not resist.

"What's next?"

This is the question that I am sure many of you have been asking since the wonderful events of your Solstice, because, Dear Hearts, that is a Human trait. Living as you do within a linear time system you are constantly thinking *"What's next?"*, for you see, Humans very rarely take the time to appreciate, to honour and to enjoy the miracles and wondrous events that occur within your lives, for in linear time it is all so rushed, whatever 'happens', suddenly becomes yesterday.

You may sit with friends and enjoy a beautiful meal, and an hour later your mind is saying *"what's next?"*, for you are forever looking forward with expectations. So it does not surprise me - it does not surprise any of your Spirit friends - that after the majestic Magenta event of the Solstice you have not taken the time to adequately embrace and honour what was *the greatest event that has happened upon the Earth Planet since it began.*

In your linear time the days have moved on, the hours have moved on, the minutes have moved on, that is all behind you and you are asking *"what's next?"*. So it may surprise you, Dear Hearts, that I have come here tonight to tell you. when you ask the question *"what's next?"* I will say *"NOTHING"*, because that is the reality of the immense changes that took place at your Solstice, the Earth itself moved into a New Dimensional Frequency, one it had never been in before, and all of Humanity upon the Earth Planet has also moved into a New Dimensional Frequency that Humanity has never been in before, so *there are no plans, no diagrams, no maps to show you what is ahead, it is just a blank page waiting to be written upon.*

So when you sit and ask *"what comes next?"* I say *"NOTHING"*, for *nothing WILL come until YOU choose to create it within your Hearts!*

Think back, Dear Hearts, in your history, to the times of someone like Columbus who set out on a ship, had no idea where he was going. Oh, he had thoughts and plans and concepts which had come from past experiences, but he had to create something completely new upon his journey, his journey of discovery, and as you may well recall he did not turn up at the place he thought he was going to turn up. This is the way it has been throughout your history, Dear Hearts, when momentous events happen, it is invariably being written on blank pages.

This is the most momentous journey you have ever undertaken and as you look out in front of yourselves you see "nothing", for "nothing" exists. Why is this so? Dear Hearts, it is because you are looking in the wrong direction, you do not look out ahead of you at the blankness, the "nothingness", you look instead into your own Hearts and you ask your own Heart *"what will I create in this New Dimensional Frequency? What will the Earth create for itself in this New Dimensional Frequency?"*

The Earth has opened its Heart, has released the Magenta Light of Love and Peace, so we know that the Earth intends to create Love and Peace on ITS journey in the New Dimensional Frequency, in its new position in the cosmos, but what are you going to create, Dear Hearts?

I refer back to the meal, you have enjoyed a beautiful meal with all your friends and you have moved away from the table, not everyone will feel hungry again at the same time - some may last an hour or two before they ask *"what's next?"* Some may last until the next day before they ask *"what's next?"* but all eventually will ask that same question, *"what's next?"*

So not all of Humanity will begin to create the new future at the same time, but all will contribute to the future when the time is right for them, when they can look into their Hearts and see the vision of **Love and Peace**, and if they cannot find that vision, Dear Hearts, they will not journey onwards with the **New Earth Planet**, for the Earth Planet has made its position totally clear, *it has opened its Heart and raised itself into the Magenta Dimension of Peace and Love,* and you have aided in that process.

Some may feel their job is now done and they can go *'Home'*, others may feel that their job is just beginning for they so want to be a part of creating the *New Magenta Earth.*

When you focus on your Hearts, you will find the time to honour and appreciate the majesty and the miracles that each 'NOW' moment provides. Do not be in such a rush to move on to the next step, to constantly ask "what's next?, what's next?, what's next?"

Focus on your Heart, embrace what is within your Heart, and when the time is right for you, your Heart will guide you, will enable you to begin to fill in the blank page that the Solstice gifted to each and every one of you.

Sometimes you wonder why it is that from time to time all the Masters come together at Shambhala and I tell you, Dear Hearts, it is because we take the time to appreciate and honour every wonderful happening upon the Earth, and in this New Dimensional Frequency, this Magenta Earth, we ask you to do the same, to move within your own Hearts and take the time to honour yourself, to honour your journey, and to find the Love and the Peace that will paint the canvas of your future with the *New Magenta Earth.*

I embrace you with deepest Love.

"What's next?"

(6th July 2015)

26

EMBRACE WHO YOU ARE <u>NOW</u>

(The Circle opens with the Sounds of the Tibetan bowls, the Blessings Chimes and the Tingsha Bells.)

Feel the vibrational frequencies moving through your body with each beat of Earth Mother's Heart, embrace the Love and the Joy that the Sound vibrations create within you and radiate through you, for it is through the Sound of Earth Mother's Heart beat that you create the new Ascension Light frequencies to enable you to progress along your pathway of Ascension.

Dear Hearts, you need in each moment to know and acknowledge your connectedness to Earth Mother, for it is through her Love and her Light that you will find the seeds of growth for yourselves. When you move out into your natural world and listen to the Sounds of the wind in your trees, or you stand by the shoreline and listen to the Sound of the waves caressing the earth, all these things are Earth Mother's Blessing to you, and when you allow them to become a part of you, you feel the upliftment of Joy.

Greetings, Dear Hearts, I am Djwahl Khul.

It is so important at this time for you to reaffirm your connectedness with Earth Mother, with the Planet on which you live, for it is within the embrace of the Earth that all growth begins. As you look around you will see that Earth Mother herself is beginning to shake off the drudgery of the past, the painfulness of past abuses. This is not something to be feared, Dear Hearts, although it is normal for Humans to fear natural events like volcanoes erupting or the Earth shaking, but this is all a part of the journey of growth for the Earth Planet - and through the Earth Planet, your own growth.

If you take the time for a moment to look back upon your own lives for the last 10 of your Earth years, or 20 of your Earth years, and look at the changes that have taken place during that time and remember how fearful and unsettled you were when some of those changes took place, then look where you are now, and you know that all those changes were necessary for you to **BE** in the position you are in now on your journey of growth.

It may well be, Dear Hearts, that in some instances you are still holding on to aspects of the past that you should have let go, so like Earth you need from time to time to shake yourself, to shake it off, to *let go of any energies of the past that are no longer relevant to your journey, that are no longer comfortable in your new frequencies of Light and Love.*

Yes, Dear Hearts, we know how difficult it is for Humans to let go of what they perceive as 'memories', for *in their memories they perceive their worthiness,* their own history, but the reality, Dear Hearts, is that 'now' is all that matters, this *"NOW moment"* is one that you have been working towards, so you may express gratitude for what has happened upon your journey, that does not mean that you have to hold on to those memories, for often within those memories the discomfort of the changes that took place are still held, and still impact on your physical vessel.

You have already been told that this is going to be a year of change on an individual level and on a collective level. The most important way that you can deal with these changes is to *embrace who you are NOW,* embrace it with Love, embrace it with Respect, embrace it with Joy. It does not matter what road you took, how long you took, all that matters is the *"NOW moment"* that you are in, for this is where you were always meant to be, where you chose to be when you chose to come to the Earth at this time.

Let go of the doubting, let go of the judgments of yourself, for those judgments are based upon those memories. Embrace the freedom of the *"NOW moment"* and know that you will move forward into higher and higher Dimensional Frequencies, if only you continue to embrace the *NOW* moment and look forward, not backwards. To let go of memories is not to let go of the reality of who you are, you are simply letting go of the images of your journey, for they are no longer there, Dear Hearts, they no longer exist, what exists is the *"NOW moment"* - the Love, the Joy, the Peace that you hold within your Heart now.

Once you have let go of the anchors of the past you will be ready to soar into the Cosmos, to soar into higher and higher Dimensional Frequencies. Give thanks, express gratitude for the journey that you have undertaken to this point in time, but do not dwell upon it, sit within your Heart and look ahead and you will see doors opening in front of you,

you will see Dimensional veils moving aside, for *once you let go of the judgments of your past, you acknowledge the worthiness of your "NOW"* and it is from within that worthiness that you will be able to step forward in the new energies, and you will be able to work with the new energies unencumbered by feelings of unworthiness, by judgments of your past, by guilt, by whatever you feel when you look back upon a journey which has been completed.

We have all shared with you some of that journey, but we do not dwell upon that, Dear Hearts, we exist only in the now and we embrace you only in the *NOW.*
We embrace who you are, not who you were.

Let go of all the energies that are no longer relevant to the *"NOW moment"* and you will feel enlightened instantly and you will feel your Heart filling with the energies of Joy, uplifting you, and you are ready for the next phase of your journey.

It is so important at this time, Dear Hearts. to let go with gratitude, with Love, releasing everything that no longer serves you in your new frequency of Love.

This is what Mother Earth is doing, this is what you also need to be doing, so that together you can move onward and upward into your true reality of Light, Love and Peace.

(25th January 2016)

27

YOU ARE FREE AT LAST, FREE TO BE

(The Circle opens with the Sounds of the Tibetan Bowls and the Tingsha bells)

As the Sound vibrations fill your Being, place your attention between your Heart and your Thymus, at the place of your *Soul Heart*, and allow yourselves to move deeply into your *Soul Heart*, that you may be uplifted in Light vibrations, to give yourselves an Eagle's view of the Earth at this time.

Sitting high in the Seat of your Soul, look out across the Earth and ***BREATHE - BREATHE*** the Peace and the Love and the Joy within your *Soul Heart* out across the Earth, caressing every part of the Earth, every Being upon the Earth.

BREATHE YOUR LOVE, and feel the vibrations of Joy, Love and Peace begin to reverberate throughout the Earth, and return as a gift to your *Soul Heart*, creating the Oneness of purpose for this time of the great shift, for it is a time of coming together in

Oneness, a time of accepting the Blessings of the Earth, and a time of embracing the Earth with your Blessings.

Feel yourself seated deep within your **Soul Heart**, vibrating at a higher frequency than ever before, knowing that you are now One with all that is.

Greetings Dear Hearts, I am Djwahl Khul, and I come tonight to sit within your **Soul Heart** - with each and every one of you - to allow you to see and feel that we are all **One** together in the new frequencies of the Earth.

For yes, Dear Ones, although you have been given dates to focus upon, the transitions are already taking place within the Earth, and within you. It is a time of lifting yourself from your Heart Chakra into your Soul Chakra, and to look out and see, and feel, and hear the intensity of frequencies that are now taking place within the Earth as it lifts into its new Dimensional frequency.

All of us in the Spirit Realms, and all of you in the Human Consciousness are now sitting at the same table. We are all part of the **one**, and we come together now with greater knowing and greater understanding of our place in the Universe, the place of the Earth within the Universe, and the place of each and every one of us within the Universe.

As you sit within your Soul Heart, you are not encumbered by all that has gone before. You are free at last, free to be, free to be.

In the new Earth frequency you will no longer be judged by what you do, but the way you are. For you are now *'of Light'*, and simply *Being* will create the Joy, the Love, the Harmony, and the Peace - for you will not feel in every moment of every day that you are in competition with others.

You will know that you are simply all a part of the One. You will be set free simply to *BE*. That is the essence of Ascension, Dear Hearts, setting yourselves free, simply to *BE.*

Take a moment to allow those words to resonate through every part of your Being, and feel the sense of Joy and Bliss welling up inside you as you realize the truth of who you are, and you acknowledge the beauty of who you are, and you acknowledge the Love that is everything - the Earth, the Oceans, the Animals, Humanity - *ALL ARE LOVE !*

So give yourselves permission, Dear Hearts, simply to **BE,** and let the Light of that Beingness flow out into the world as your contribution to the whole.

(17th December 2012)

28

THE WHOLE PICTURE IS ONE OF GREAT DIVINE LOVE

(The Circle opens with the Sounds of the Tibetan Bowls)

Allow the Sounds of the bowls to lift you up into your Soul Dimension, feeling yourself being filled with Divine Light.

Greetings Dear Hearts, I am Djwahl Khul.

We are aware at this time of transition on the Earth Planet that it is easy for you to become disheartened and disillusioned as you look out upon the Earth and see the images of chaos and darkness swirling around the Planet, and you may be crying deep within your Heart 'where is the Peace?, where is the Love?, where is the Joy that we perceived would come when the Ascension of the Earth and of Humanity began to take place?'

Well, Dear Hearts, I am here tonight to tell you that nothing is as it seems on the surface of the Earth at this time. The Peace, the Love, the Joy and the Light are filling your Planet, even though they are not yet filling your minds and your eyes.

Most of you at some stage will have put together a jigsaw puzzle, so I ask you now to imagine a table in front of you with jigsaw pieces scattered around the table - let us say 5,000 jigsaw pieces - and someone comes along and picks up one piece of the jigsaw puzzle and holds it in front of your eyes, and by so doing invites you to form a judgment on what the total picture of this jigsaw puzzle is.

The piece chosen may be filled with bright Light and you may imagine that the whole picture must therefore be bright, joyful, beautiful. Equally the piece chosen to be placed before your eyes may be totally black, and you may imagine that the full picture will be dark and somber, but I know that as I create this picture for you, you will perhaps laugh, or shake your head knowing that you cannot possibly imagine the full picture from one small piece of the jigsaw, and yet, Dear Hearts, this is precisely what is happening with you at this time.

The images being drawn to your attention on your television screens, on your radios, in your newspapers, are one or two or three small pieces of the jigsaw of your Planet, and you know in your minds and in your Hearts that often these pieces are carefully selected with the intention of creating certain reactions within **YOU**, and you are invited to perceive the 'whole of the Earth' through these small pieces of your jigsaw.

And, all too often, you fall into the trap of accepting that invitation to perceive the whole from just one small piece of the jigsaw puzzle, and at this stage much of what you are being shown is of the chaos, of the darkness, of the unrest upon your Planet, both within Humanity and indeed within the Planet itself.

You see images of floods, but only in small areas of the Earth - you do not see the rest of the Earth, you are not shown the rest of the Earth. You are shown fighting in certain countries of the Earth, but you are not shown the rest of the Earth where people are living joyfully, happily together, peaceful. No you are not shown that, Dear Hearts, you are shown selective pieces of the jigsaw puzzle, and because you cannot see the rest of the puzzle, you try to react to what you are shown.

Of course, when you did your jigsaw puzzles in the past the pieces usually came in a box and on the cover of the box was a representation of the whole of what your jigsaw puzzle would look like, but where the Earth is concerned Dear Hearts there is no box, there is no image of the complete picture, there are only the pieces of the jigsaw puzzle.

You need, Dear Ones, to realize this, and to move yourselves up into your Soul Dimension and look at other pieces of the jigsaw puzzle that you may view from that Higher Perspective. Expand your view beyond the one small piece of the jigsaw puzzle that is being presented to you on your television screen or in your newspapers.

Know in your Heart that there is more to life, more to the Earth than meets the eye in that one small piece of the jigsaw puzzle, and *know* in your Heart that what you are not seeing is more important than what you are being shown. And *know* with great certainty and great belief that what you are not being shown is in truth what will create the new Earth, the Peace, the Love, the Harmony, the Joy. It is everywhere on the Earth Planet. It is everywhere within that jigsaw puzzle.

You do not need to see the whole picture, you simply need to KNOW that the whole picture is one of great Divine Love, and allow that knowledge to guide your steps, to lift your emotions, to feel and see the reality of Peace and Love on Earth.

Do not limit yourselves to those individual pieces of the jigsaw puzzle. Expand yourself, expand your Heart and embrace the whole of the Earth as a place of Peace and Joy, and as you perceive the Earth in this Light, it will become that Earth, and the individual pieces of the jigsaw puzzle will slowly be fitted together to create the wholeness, the wondrous wholeness of the new Earth.

Each piece of the jigsaw puzzle represents a single Heart on the Earth Planet coming together to create the whole. Not every Heart is filled with Light at this time, Dear Ones, you know that, but once they come together and bind together, they will create the new Earth of Peace and Love.

(19th August 2013)

29

REMAIN WITHIN THE 'TRUTH OF YOUR HEART'

(The Gathering opens with the Sounds of the Blessings Chimes, the Tibetan Bowls and the Drum)

Allow yourselves to take three deep breaths, holding each one for a moment then expelling it out into the World carrying with it the vibrations of Love from deep within your Hearts.

Greetings, Dear Hearts, I am Djwahl Khul

I am overjoyed to be with you in this special *"Sacred Space"*, where the energies of Love are no longer confined, but are open to all, and where each one of you lets go of any barriers you have been holding to your Light and your Love radiating forth out into the World, for *this is a time upon the Earth Planet when the maximum amount of Light and Love needs to be circulated freely.*

You are seeing much through your Media of the chaos that is taking place in different parts of the World, and it is all too easy to withdraw into yourselves, to feel that you are only safe if you close yourself off to what is happening upon the Earth, but, Dear Hearts, that is not the way to go. What is needed is more and more Light, more and more Love radiating from the Hearts of all those who have awakened to the reality of Ascension upon and within the Earth Planet.

The more negativity that is radiated out into the World by your Global Media, and by your Social Media, the more Light and Love is required to balance those energies.

Fear is an energy of the past, it has no place in the Higher Frequencies of Light, so do not allow those energies of fear to lock you away from the rest of Humanity and from the Earth Itself. Open *More*, for it is your Love and your Light that will counterbalance the waves of fear that those who seek to be in charge and in control of your lives are sending out at this time.

Dear Hearts, it is important to remember that much of what you are hearing and seeing at this time is not

'Truth', is not *'Fact'*, it is all too often speculation. You see an event shown on your TV screens instantly, because of your new Media, but you do not know the truth of what is happening, for immediately it is shown upon your TV screens so called experts are called in to postulate and speculate, and they build castles around a *'Grain of Sand'*, and it is up to you, Dear Hearts, to recognize that what you are looking at is a *'Grain of Sand'* and not the castles that many of these people are seeking to build.

If you focus upon that *'Grain of Sand'* and send it Love and Light, the castle collapses around it, and you begin to see the kernels of *'Truth'* emerging. Unfortunately, Dear Hearts, you live in a time upon your Earth Planet of what you call '24 hour news cycles', and of course your Social Media, where everything that happens is captured and sent out further, and added to.

Most of you, Dear Hearts, will recall as you were growing up you played games, and you may have played a game which some called *"Whispers"*, where you were told a story, and you then had to tell that story to someone else, and they in turn had to tell that story to someone else again, and it went that way around the circle until it came back and was whispered into your ear once more, and I'm sure that you will recall, Dear Hearts, that what came back to you was not what you sent out originally. It had not necessarily been deliberately corrupted or changed, it was simply that in passing it on some people omitted parts of it, or added flavor to it, so that when the story came back and was whispered into your ear, it bore no relationship to the **'Truth'** that began the Whisper.

Do you recall this, Dear Hearts ?

This is what is happening in your World now, the **'Grain of Sand'** sends out a message, others pick it up, embellish it, speculate upon it, change it, and when it goes out into the darkest parts of the World it is a new 'monster of fear', because you are no longer seeing the **'Grain of Sand'**. So remember, Dear Hearts, when these vistas of fear arrive in your minds let your Hearts radiate Love, and dispel the darkness, and move that Love and that Light from within you out into the World so that these constructed illusions, these castles of fear, can be dissipated by the **'Truth'** of **Love,** of **Peace,** of **Joy** and of **Harmony**.

For in reality, Dear Hearts, those things are the only 'Truth' upon the Earth – Love, Peace, Joy, Harmony. These are the *'Truths'*, the rest is the darkness of illusion seeking to prevent the *'Truth'* from being realized.

Beloved Germain suggested that you embrace *'Silliness'* on a daily basis, this is to encourage the Joy and the Love, the Peace and the Harmony within you, so that you can maintain that energy at all times, even when you are surrounded by these illusions of fear, for if you remain within the *'Truth of your Heart'*, the rest of the World will begin to change - for *Love* and *Peace* overwhelm the illusions of fear.

Dear Hearts, I thank you for being with me at this time, I know that you are embracing your Ceremony for the Waters of the World, and it is important that you do so from the **Truth within your own Hearts.**

Blessings be upon you.

(22nd July 2016)

30

LOVING YOURSELF IS A PRIORITY IN ORDER TO LOVE OTHERS

(The Circle opens with the Sounds of the Tibetan bowls and the Blessings Chimes.)

Embrace the special energies of the Blessings Chimes, imagine it as standing under a shower with the vibrational frequencies of Blessings pouring down onto your body, filling you completely with the energy of Blessings, and as you store those energies within yourself, cast those Blessings out onto the Earth to embrace each and every Being of Light, and to create a vision of Love within the Hearts of all Humanity.

It is the Love within your Hearts that moves away the darkness of fear, the darkness of anger, the darkness of judgment. So feel the Blessings that you are, and share your Blessings with the world.

Greetings Dear Hearts, I am Djwahl Khul.

This is a time of great upheaval on the Earth Planet, the last vestiges of darkness seeking to retain their power over Humanity. *The last vestiges of darkness* - for there are now too many upon the Earth who live in the Love within their Hearts, and that *Love creates a brightness of Light that the darkness of the past cannot resist,* so do not look out upon your world and be depressed by what you see, for what you see or what you are being allowed to see is only a very small part of the story of the Earth at this time.

There are so many wonderful, beautiful things happening upon your Planet that you do not see, that you are unaware of - on the surface - but deep within the Love within your Hearts, *You Know, You See, You Feel all the positive, wonderful, beautiful happenings upon the Earth.*

From time to time, Dear Hearts, these creep through onto your television screens, you see Humanity come together to save a whale, beached, and you know that this is a beautiful oneness of sharing, but it is not isolated in the way that you are led to believe, it is happening more and more in different parts of your world, Humans and animals interacting, Humans and nature interacting with positive results.

The focus of your media is always the story that tugs upon your Hearts the most, and those are invariably tales of sadness and darkness.

Look beyond and see and feel the Light and the Love that is building upon the Earth at this time. *Feel it within your own Heart, know that you are BEING and SEEING Light, Joy, Happiness all around you.*

Take a moment, Dear Hearts, to sit and remember how things used to be for you before you found the Love within your Hearts, and how those things have changed so radically over recent years in your linear time, how you have grown into beautiful non-judgmental Human Beings.

You have accepted that loving yourself is a priority in order to Love others. You were told when you were growing up perhaps, that loving yourself was selfish, self-centred, you should always put other people ahead of yourself. This was the controlling of humanity.

Love and Light has set you free, free to Love yourself and through that Love to embrace others, to share openly and honestly with others, from the purity of the Love within your Hearts, and this, Dear Hearts, will grow and grow.

The darkness is fading - Love and Light are taking root upon the Earth and creating change more quickly than ever before.

Remain steadfast in Love, and through that Love you will create the Peace that you have only dreamed of in the past, a Peace that respects the Love and the Joy within all other Beings, a Peace that accepts differences as uniqueness, not as threats, for Love is truly Oneness.

You have created that Oneness within yourselves, now it is time to show that Oneness and allow others to feel your Love, your Joy, your Harmony.

(28th July 2014)

GLOSSARY

Ascended Masters - Spiritually Enlightened Beings who have previously incarnated in Human form on the Earth but who are now in Higher Dimensional Frequencies.

Wesak – A celebration of the Birth, Enlightenment and Ascension of the Buddha.

Shambhala - A 'City of Light' in Higher Dimensional frequencies where Spiritual and Cosmic Beings work together in Oneness. Some perceive it to be situated Energetically above the Wesak Valley in Tibet. Channeled information given to me indicates that Shambhala is a structure within the Etheric comprised of 6 energy Pyramids of the 4 sided variety, connected together to form the Sacred Geometric shape of a Merkaba.

Pendragon – When David J Adams moved house in 2006 he was told in a dream that the House would be called 'Pendragon', so from that time his Meditation Circle became known as Pendragon Meditation Circle. Pendragon, of course, was the Name given to Welsh Kings of old like Uther Pendragon (father of

Arthur of the Round Table), so could be a reflection of David's Welsh heritage.

Songlines – there are 12 major songlines throughout the Earth which come together at two places, Sundown Hill just outside Broken Hill in Australia (they are represented here by Sculptures) and Machu Picchu in Peru. They are vibrational, or Sound Arteries of the Planet.

Blessings Chimes – A hand held instrument created from wind Chimes which are used to Bless the Earth, the Oceans and all Beings of Light upon the Earth.

Crystalline Grid – A structured network of Crystals throughout the Earth that are part of the electromagnetic composition of the Earth.

Isle of Avalon – A sacred Site at Glastonbury in the United Kingdom. The Glastonbury Tor is the remnant of this Island that housed the Divine Feminine aspects of the 'old Earth' religions. It continues to exist, but in another Dimensional form and is a 'gateway' to other Dimensions. It is also regarded as the *HEART CHAKRA* of the Earth Planet.

Equinox - An **equinox** is commonly regarded as the moment when the plane of Earth's equator passes through the center of the Sun's disk, which occurs twice each year, around 20 March and 23 September. In other words, it is the point in which the center of the visible sun is directly over the equator.

Solstice - A **solstice** is an event occurring when the Sun appears to reach its most northerly or southerly excursion relative to the celestial equator on the celestial sphere. Two solstices occur annually, on about 21 June and 21 December. The seasons of the year are directly connected to both the solstices and the equinoxes.

Marine Meditation – This was a Global Meditation initiated by Beloved Germain to be held at 8pm on each Equinox, wherever people were in the world. It focused on connecting with the ***CONSCIOUSNESS OF THE OCEANS***. It ran from March 1991 to September 2012 - 22 years and 44 meditations in all. See http://www.dolphinempowerment.com/MarineMeditation.htm

Mount Kailash – Mount Kailash is a peak in the Kailash Range in Tibet. Mount Kailash is considered to be Sacred in four Religions, Buddhism, Hinduism, Bon and Jainism.

Labyrinth - A Sacred Geometric Design or Pattern that creates a Path or journey to the center, and a return along the same route. On a Spiritual level it represents a metaphor for the journey to the centre of your deepest self, and back out into the world with a broadened understanding of who you are. With a Labyrinth there is only one choice to make, that choice is to enter or not, that choice is to walk the Spiritual path in front of you, or not. The choice is always yours to make within your Heart. There is no right or wrong way to walk a Labyrinth, you only have to enter and follow the path to the Center – the Center of yourself. Walk it in **LOVE**, walk it in **PEACE** and walk it in **RESPECT.**

Eight Pointed Star Spiral Labyrinth of Creation – Front cover picture, Walked at the Marine Meditation in 2006, Carries the Harmonic note of Dragon.

SONGLINES, NAMES AND APPROXIMATE ROUTES

We have given names to the 12 Songlines that embrace the Earth Planet based on the names of the 12 Sculpture on Sundown Hill, just outside Broken Hill in New South Wales, Australia. Below we give the approximate routes that the Songlines take between Sundown Hill and Machu Picchu as they were given to us in meditation.

RAINBOW SERPENT: Sundown Hill – Willow Springs – Mount Gee (Arkaroola) – Kings Canyon (near Uluru) – Mount Kailash (Tibet) – Russia – North Pole – via the North American Spine to Machu Picchu.

MOTHERHOOD: Sundown Hill – India – South Africa – follows the Nile River to North Africa – Machu Picchu.

THE BRIDE: Sundown Hill – Pacific Rim of Fire – Machu Picchu.

MOON GODDESS: Sundown Hill – Across the Nullabor to Perth – Madagascar – Mount Kilimanjaro – Egypt (Hathor Temple) – Via the Mary Line to the United Kingdom – Machu Picchu.

BAJA EL SOL JAGUAR (UNDER THE JAGUAR SUN): Sundown Hill – Grose Valley (New South Wales) – New Zealand – Chile – Via the Spine of South America (Andes) – Machu Picchu.

ANGELS OF SUN AND MOON: Sundown Hill – Willow Springs - Curramulka (Yorke Peninsular of South Australia) – Edithburgh (also Yorke Peninsular of South Australia) - Kangaroo Island – Mount Gambier - Tasmania – South Pole - Machu Picchu.

A PRESENT TO FRED HOLLOWS IN THE AFTERLIFE: Sundown Hill – Arltunga (Central Australia) – Through the Gold Light Crystal to Brazil – along the Amazon to Machu Picchu.

TIWI TOTEMS: Sundown Hill – South Sea Islands – Hawaii – Mount Shasta (USA) – Lake Moraine (Canada) – via Eastern Seaboard of USA to Machu Picchu.

HORSE: Sundown Hill – Philippines – China – Mongolia – Tibet – Europe – France – Machu Picchu.

FACING THE NIGHT AND DAY: Sundown Hill – Queensland (Australia) – New Guinea – Japan – North

Russia to Finland – Sweden – Norway – Iceland – Tip of Greenland – Machu Picchu.

HABITAT: Sundown Hill via Inner Earth to Machu Picchu.

THOMASINA (JILARRUWI – THE IBIS): Tension Lynch pin between Sundown Hill and Machu Picchu.

HOW TO MAKE YOUR OWN BLESSINGS CHIMES

Blessings Chimes have a triangular wooden top. Inserted into the underside of the wooden triangle are a series of Screw Eyes with a series of chimes dangling from them with THREE 'Strikers' of your own design. The chimes are of different sizes, thicknesses or metals to provide a variety of Tones (which we created by taking apart a number of different, inexpensive, wind chimes). The Screw Eyes are set out in 5 rows from which the Chimes are hung, a single chime at the tip of the triangle, then 2 chimes, then 3 chimes, then 5 chimes and finally 7 chimes. This makes 18 chimes in all. One Screw Eye from which a 'Striker' hangs is placed between rows 2 and 3, and then two Screw Eyes from which 'Strikers' hang are placed between rows 4 and 5.

The 'Strikers' used in creating our Original Blessings Chime for the Marine Meditation had as decorations a Sea horse, a Unicorn, and a Dragon. The Triangular wooden top has a small knob on it, to hold as you shake the Blessings Chimes to create the vibration and resonance.

Although the original has a triangular Top and 18 chimes, you can vary this to your own intuition. The latest version that has been created for David has an Octagonal top and only 8 chimes and is called 'Peace and Harmony Chimes' rather than 'Blessings Chimes' to reflect it's more subtle Sound. Use your imagination and Intuition.

Blessings of Love and Peace

David J Adams

Printed in the United States
By Bookmasters